BOOK NO: 1751456

Supporting Readers

School and Classroom Strategies

Maggie Moore and Barrie Wade

David Fulton Publishers
London

David Fulton Publishers Ltd
2 Barbon Close, London WC1N 3JX

First published in Great Britain by David Fulton Publishers 1995

Note: The right of Maggie Moore and Barrie Wade to be identified as the authors of this work has been asserted by them in accordance with the copyright, Designs and Patents Act 1988.

Copyright © Maggie Moore and Barrie Wade

British Library Cataloguing in Publication Data

A catalogue record for this book is available from the British Library

ISBN 1-85346-372-8

Typeset by The Harrington Consultancy Ltd
Printed in Great Britain by BPC Books and Journals Ltd., Exeter

Contents

Dedication

For Dorrie

Introduction

I hate reading/you just sit there and do nothing/and if you read to the teacher/if you get it wrong you have to do it again/the books/they're for little kids/it's a waste of time.

Celine (age 10)

Celine does not enjoy reading; she finds it hard and she does not see the point of trying. She cannot understand why people read for pleasure. She is, at the age of 10, a struggling reader and, despite the help that she gets from school may well remain so. She no longer wants to learn to read. Why is this? What can be done to change her attitude and teach her the strategies that will help her to learn and to progress?

There are other children like Celine. Some struggle and just about get by. Others can read but do not choose to. Others seem unable to cope successfully with any reading task.

Children who make slow progress at reading often struggle in other areas of the curriculum. In order to take part in the majority of curriculum activities and tasks, reading is essential. Mathematics textbooks are difficult for some children, not because of the mathematical concepts they are teaching, but because explanations and instructions are written and have to be read. The gap between inexperienced readers and their peers often widens as they journey through school with a consequent negative effect on confidence, self-esteem and motivation to learn.

There are many reasons why individual children fail to make sufficient reading progress even with competent early teaching; some may have been absent at crucial stages in learning; some may continue to rely on a single reading strategy – a reliance which is not effective when reading becomes more complex; some children are not interested in the reading content (particularly if it is patronising); and others take longer to sort out the confusions which affect all early readers. In mainstream classrooms lack of progress can have many causes; it is less likely to be caused by a general learning difficulty. In this there are grounds for optimism: the effective teacher can diagnose difficulties expertly, choose appropriate learning resources and give support to individual learners.

It is essential, however, that children are given appropriate and explicit help as soon as possible. Various programmes have been shown to be effective in the early years of schooling. For example, Reading Recovery is an intervention programme for children in their second year of school and has been very successful (Simmons, 1991; Wade and Moore, 1993). Reading Recovery teaches children necessary strategies to solve the puzzle of reading and makes writing an integral component of the sessions.

Intervention for struggling readers at Key Stage 2, however, is more likely to employ a skills based programme rather than an organic approach involving writing, speaking and listening and access to challenging books. Our preliminary research for the study which we report here found only six schools out of 46 that used an integrated approach rather than a skills based reading programme with struggling readers older than seven years of age.

The traditional approach to reading difficulty with strugglers placed in remedial groups has been shown to be ineffective, since the reading gains made are not sustained once the child returns to the normal classroom (for example, Collins, 1961; Cashdan and Pumfrey, 1969). Some insightful approaches have been successful with individuals (Meek, 1983; Martin, 1989). Such help, even though successful, is not part of ordinary classroom activity and may be perceived as separate from the language work of the class. An approach is needed, which is essentially a whole class approach, but one that can also be used with the inexperienced reader using the peer group for support. Skills learning is necessary, but indications are that learning of skills is likely to be most effective in a context of enjoyment and response to literature. The purpose of this book is to investigate the possibilities and effectiveness of such an approach.

We begin by examining the different approaches to teaching inexperienced readers beyond the age of seven. We then report the findings of our own West Midlands study of reading progress and discuss its implications for teaching and learning. Thus, Chapter 1 outlines current approaches to teaching struggling readers, while Chapter 2 focuses specifically on what we have called an integrated approach. In Chapter 3 we describe the background of our research. There follow several chapters in which we present the results of our study. Chapter 4 presents quantitative findings on reading age, comprehension and intonation. Chapter 5 focuses on fluency in reading, Chapter 6 on children's attitudes and response to literature and Chapter 7 presents a digest of opinions from learners themselves. Chapter 8 outlines with illustrations the strategies used in this research and indicates their possibilities for incorporation into a school reading programme. Chapter 9 reviews the research and considers implications for schools.

CHAPTER ONE
Teaching Reading Strategies

On a huge hill
Cragged and steep, truth stands, and hee that will
Reach her, about must, and about must goe;
And what the hill's suddenness resists, winne so
John Donne

Introduction

For John Donne the search for truth is neither simple nor straightforward. This is particularly so when the field of discovery is huge. Reading has been described as the 'patterning of complex behaviour' (Clay, 1979). Good readers perceive the pattern; others, however, see it revealed only partially. This chapter briefly describes the reading process, then evaluates researchers' views on providing for inexperienced readers beyond the age of seven. This analysis leads to a review of some of the ways schools provide for what they describe as children with difficulties in reading.

The Reading Process

Inexperienced readers need systematic help to perceive and understand that the complex pattern of reading involves complex levels of response. The Bullock Report (DES, 1975) described this complexity in three levels:

a response to graphic symbols in terms of the words they represent *plus*

a response to text in terms of the meanings that the author intends to set down *plus*

a response to the author's meanings in terms of all relevant previous experience and present judgement of the reader
(p.79, para. 6.5).

Reading is not a passive process where the reader merely assimilates what is on the page, but is an activity requiring interaction between the reader of the text and the text itself. As the Cox Report (DES and WO, 1988) clearly states:

> Reading is much more than the decoding of black marks on a page; it is a quest for meaning and one which requires the reader to be an active participant. (p.40, para. 9.4)

The interactive nature of the reading process implies that readers make multiple responses to texts. For example, they decode, read for meaning, criticise and employ their previous experience of life and of other texts.

Within the decoding process readers discriminate letter and word shapes, recognise letter strings, recognise individual words and use short and long term memory processes to retain what has been decoded. But readers also need to know how a text works (for example, that in English the words go from left to right and down the page), have to understand the purpose and meaning of the reading task and have to use semantic and syntactic cues to anticipate and predict. They also need to review what they have read to enable them to understand and to use their past experience to make sense of the content. Perhaps it is surprising that so many youngsters learn to read at all!

Inexperienced Readers: Research perspectives

To be effective the teaching of reading needs to reflect these interactive processes of decoding, comprehension and personal response. Researchers such as Holdaway (1980) and Daneman (1987) recognise the necessity for a range of strategies to interpret the interdependent cues within a reading text. However, teaching in schools may not always be so enlightened. History has shown (Michael, 1987; Moore and Wade, 1995) that teaching methods often emphasise one set of processes, relegating others to secondary and minor positions of importance. For example, over many years there was argument about the right way to teach reading, which polarised the approaches of phonics and word recognition. Both of these approaches emphasised decoding skills and were hierarchical and sequential, suggesting that learning to read was a linear road to progression. More recently the argument has been whether skills or meaning was the 'right' way.

Whatever the approach used for the majority of readers in a particular school, the skills approach traditionally has been the way to teach struggling readers (Jansen, 1985) even when they have already failed to learn to read through this approach. The assumption remains that struggling readers require the acquisition of skills in a rigidly prescribed order. Furthermore, the sequential nature of skills acquisition is frequently broken down into very small steps in the belief that this is necessary for success.

For many inexperienced readers beyond the age of seven, therefore, whole word learning is restricted to a basic vocabulary introduced gradually through a series of books in a reading scheme. Sounds of letters of the alphabet are taught in sequential progression, as is the blending of two or more letter sounds to make phonically regular words. Such an approach to the teaching of reading is firmly based on behaviourist principles of step-by-step learning in order to shape behaviour (Skinner, 1969 and 1972) and repetition to produce a conditioned response (Thorndike, 1931) to the stimulus of a flash card, for example. The reading process is broken down into apparently manageable parts, mastered separately and then finally put together in context. Whilst the intention is to simplify reading and learning for the inexperienced reader, many educationalists (for example, Blank, 1985; Smith, 1982) argue that it makes reading much more difficult. Goodman (1986) maintains that the breaking of language into bits and pieces is artificial and irrelevant to the learner, because language is used out of context and seems to serve no discernible purpose. The lack of concentration on reading for meaning and understanding removes what is essential to the young reader: the communicative purpose of reading. After all, the greater the number of steps, the harder it is to see where you are supposed to be going!

Proponents of a step-by-step skills approach do not always ignore factors of context, meaning and understanding, although they are sometimes introduced last and have less emphasis. Beech (1985), for example, suggests that phonics and a small sight vocabulary are combined into meaningful sentences to allow understanding to take place, but argues that reading for meaning and understanding come after automatic decoding is established. His argument is that children think consciously only of decoding, but this is by no means proven.

A frequently advocated step-by-step approach is that of phonics. Phonics requires the sub-skills of being able to look at a word, analyse each grapheme (letter), translate each into a phoneme (sound) and then synthesise (blend) the phonemes into a word. Phonics teaching and learning invariably follow a hierarchical sequence, moving from individual letter sounds to blends and eventually to words. Sometimes phonics teaching for struggling readers has been more blatant than in initial teaching. Tansley (1976), for example, suggested that teaching phonics to 'backward readers' should be more finely graded than in initial teaching. He suggested separating the letters for blending a word such as 'ran' into r-a-n, rather than producing an initial blend such as ra-n or r-an.

Unfortunately, such a process further isolates sounds from words and takes the learners away from a meaningful context.

Many studies have sought to demonstrate the effectiveness of phonic training on reading ability, though few of these have focussed on inexperienced readers beyond the age of seven. For example, Harding, Beech and Sneddon (1985), after examining oral reading errors of British school children, give support for increasing grapheme to phoneme knowledge. Beech (1987), however, recognises that such processing gives way to a whole word approach by readers and that the majority develop a combination of strategies to acquire meaning from text. Research of this kind argues for phonics as a first stage in the reading process, but this is not helpful for the minority of older children still working to acquire effective strategies. Struggling readers often rely on the one strategy that they have been taught (Barr, 1972), usually phonics, and may not develop the range of strategies necessary to acquire meaning unless they get specific encouragement and guidance.

The prevalence and dominance of phonics teaching have been criticised even by those who fully endorse its usefulness. Durkin (1965) stresses the importance of phonics in reading instruction but states (p.16) that it is only one aspect of reading and that it should not be emphasised at the expense of others. Naidoo (1981) recommends phonic teaching and a highly structured approach for teaching dyslexic children, but stresses the importance of reading, writing and spelling being learned together rather than as isolated skills. She strongly recommends that books are read to children. Chall (1983) after reviewing 67 research studies suggests that 'code emphases' are better than 'meaning emphases'. Later, however, she reports that they should not be taught as isolated skills, but in the context of challenging books (Chall, 1990). Other researchers give less primacy to phonics. Merritt (1985) endorses phonics teaching but relegates it to second place in the teaching of reading. First place is reserved for helping children to make better use of context which gives them opportunities for solving phonic problems by making use of the familiarity of patterns and possibilities of language. Southgate (1985) argues similarly, emphasising the importance of context cues before phonic skills. Hudson (1988), while stressing the need to learn about sound/symbol correspondence, also criticises the boring and nonsensical tasks that children have to do in graded phonic schemes.

It seems that reliance on phonic strategies often requires a great deal of unproductive work by the struggling reader, particularly when skills are taught in isolation. Goodman (1986) suggests that children with reading difficulties who receive additional isolated drills for phonics and word attack skills have less time for learning language and using language to learn. He also suggests (1992) that reducing the teaching of reading, writing and spelling to 'simple skills sequence' (p.197) isolates what is learned from how the language is used.

In fact, children who attempt to sound out every word have an almost impossible task in acquiring sense and meaning from the text:

> ...children sacrifice meaning and reality on the altar of faith in a word attack system which they have not mastered. (Arnold, 1990, p.210)

A knowledge of letter–sound associations alone does not lead to success in reading or spelling for children with 'reading difficulties' (Cateldo and Ellis, 1990); neither does it take into account children's learning preferences. Huxford, Terrell and Bradley (1991), for example, show that young readers can often give the sounds of letters in words they are asked to read but are unable to connect the letters in order to make the word. Bryant and Bradley (1985) observe that children can read the words they cannot write and write words they cannot read. They suggest this discrepancy is because children prefer to read by 'look and say' and prefer to write by phonics.

A balanced view is expressed by Adams (1990) in a review of current research on learning to read. She argues for the importance of phonic instruction in developing phonological awareness (the recognition of sounds in words), but warns against emphasising instruction in isolation. She recommends that skills should be developed in context with real reading and real writing.

There is no doubt that phonological awareness is utilised by readers as they make sense of texts, though phonics teaching may not have contributed much to that awareness. Bradley (1990) makes the point that much phonics teaching has little to do with phonological awareness and that children with reading difficulties have not been helped by it. She states:

> In many cases it (phonics) has become a mechanistic and meaningless ritual far from reading – the 'ker-arh-ter says cat' approach, a labyrinth of elaborate programmes and rules, which must only add to the children's difficulties. (Bradley, 1990, p.84)

Instead she refers to her earlier work (Bryant and Bradley, 1985) and suggests that children should be given experience of rhyming units and shown how they work rather than by building words letter by letter. Bryant and Bradley employed direct teaching of phonological awareness to children with reading difficulties in a relevant context of story and book writing which supported the particular skills and interests of children in their sample.

Some critics are more forthright and fundamentally question the relevance of phonics teaching. Meek (1989, p.147), for example, questions whether phonics should be explicitly taught:

> Children learn phonics by reading, not reading by phonics.

Kohl (1988) suggests that phonics should be the last resort in the teaching of reading. Slim (1990) argues that overuse of phonics leads to disabled readers. Similarly, Weaver (1992, p.54) maintains that 'heavy phonics', by which she means extensive and intensive phonics, serve to keep slow learning students in their place. Phonic instruction, she argues, prevents children from thinking for themselves and achieving their potential as readers. Smith (1973, p.130) states:

> The mere fact that sound–spelling correspondence exists does not necessarily entail that they are of critical importance in either reading or writing.

Inexperienced Readers: Classroom provision

There are two sets of conclusions to be drawn from this discussion. First, it is doubtful whether specific phonics teaching helps all readers, though phonological awareness is important for developing reading strategies. Most commentators now agree that phonics teaching divorced from the context of continuous text has little value. This is true for beginning readers and also for children beyond the age of seven who are still working towards independence in reading. Secondly, it is clear that phonological awareness provides the reader with one set of cues and strategies for making meaning. However, there are other cues and strategies such as word shape, knowledge of language and context. Readers need help to use a range of cues and approaches effectively. In particular, the struggling reader who only employs phonic strategies is unlikely to make rapid progress or derive satisfaction from reading, unless given access to other strategies.

These conclusions also hold for any single skills based approach, for example, word recognition. Skills based approaches work 'bottom up' starting with sub-skills (for example, letter sounds then words) and only gradually moving towards texts which demand understanding or response. Many reading schemes have a carefully controlled vocabulary and provide resources for learning new words in isolation (flash cards) and only later practising them in context.

The assumption of a word recognition skills approach is that children are taught a sight vocabulary through flash cards – single words presented individually which they 'read' and remember. There is, however, no guarantee that the child is focusing on the print when learning the words. Recognising the word 'house' by an ink stain in the corner of the flash card may explain why some children find the transition from flash card to text problematic. It is simply a visual memory test – and there is much more to reading than that, as we have already pointed out.

Many reading programmes used in schools are problematic, particularly if they are based on a single skills approach. The systematic organisation of materials seems to imply finely graded progress, but this is not guaranteed. Many of the earlier (but still used) schemes have been criticised for the paucity of language which a strictly controlled, repetitive and limited vocabulary frequently results in. They have also been criticised for artificial language structures different from natural patterns, so that children have a difficult, unsupported task (Wade, 1990), for lack of narrative and story content (Spencer, 1976), for lack of interest (Lapp and Flood, 1978), for boring repetition, vacuous content (Bettelheim and Zelan, 1991). Most seriously, such materials present the reader with a restricted view of reading. Many scheme books, particularly in the crucial early stages and in materials designed specifically for 'remedial reading', are stripped of language in the mistaken belief that this makes reading easier. They seem to work from the premise that children bring nothing to the task of learning to read. Children do, however, bring a wide range of knowledge of vocabulary and syntactic structure (Somerfield, Torbe and Wood, 1983), of rhyme and rhythm (Minns, 1990) and a strong sense of narrative (Wade, 1984) all of which can be used to give support in learning to read. When, however, children meet a book where the language is stilted, where enforced repetition disobeys story conventions (for example, non-use of the past tense) then the richness of their previous language and learning experiences cannot be used and reading becomes a problem.

Simplification of the text produces difficulties as it leads to the omission of essential 'non-context' words which provide the connective features of the text (Blank, 1985). Words such as 'but', 'so', 'then' and 'until' which relate ideas to each other, provide useful cues to the cohesive factors within the text and ultimately to the understanding of the author's intent.

It is sometimes argued that bottom up reading programmes are designed for teachers rather than for children. Much depends on how they are used. The structured sequence can be disadvantageous, if competition encourages children to race through books ahead of their peers. In this case, very negative messages are conveyed as to what reading is about. One child in our study, Brendan, said: 'I've got to read three more and I'm finished.' His view of reading is that it would be over and done with once the scheme was completed. Competition is likely to have an even more serious effect on inexperienced readers who perceive themselves way behind their peers. Competition does not always motivate or encourage children to work harder; many inexperienced readers beyond the age of seven are in danger of giving up because they wish to avoid failure.

In the real world books are not designed to be raced through. Ordinary reading involves the reader engaging with the text, making meaning, reflecting, understanding plot or information, re-reading for enjoyment and pleasure or to find specific information. Reading schemes are often not designed to be re-read – unless, of course, it is decided that the child has failed and needs the practice. In this case poor motivation and poor progress are compounded by material which is perceived as boring and patronising.

Being a reader is more than having the ability to decode text. Many of the children between the ages of seven and nine have acquired decoding skills, but could not be described as effective readers. A reader is someone who is able to read meaningfully and is willing to do so. Lutrario (1990, p.17) suggests that being an effective reader is partly a matter of skill and partly of attitude. Children who have positive attitudes towards reading are more likely to be motivated to learn, persevere and extend their learning (Moon and Rabin, 1980).

The teaching of skills to children with difficulties must be done in a meaningful context of interesting, supportive yet challenging books. Such children have a varied experience of language which can be brought to a text to be shared. Choate and Rakes (1989) specifically refer to the necessity of integrating the language arts where children learn to read and write simultaneously, aided by discussion, and the need to teach reading as a thinking process.

Summary

This chapter has described the processes involved in reading and has reflected upon and analysed the skills approach to teaching these processes. Skills teaching has been shown to be insufficient by itself, both for the beginning and older, inexperienced reader. The child who is still working towards independence in reading is best supported by natural, meaningful texts and teaching which integrates reading, writing, speaking and listening. The next chapter focuses upon the ways that an integrated language approach helps to support inexperienced readers.

CHAPTER TWO
The Integrated Approach to Reading

Teachers should realise that reading is a complex but unitary process and not a set of discrete skills which can be taught separately and, ultimately, bolted together.

(DES and WO, 1989, para. 16.9)

Introduction

The integrated approach to the teaching of reading that we discuss in this chapter is the antithesis of the hierarchical, skills based, schematic approach which teaches skills in isolation and ultimately attempts to 'bolt them together'. It does not use solely graded material which is simplified through a controlled vocabulary or rely exclusively on phonic patterns. It does not isolate reading and writing instruction from their role in learning.

Instead it is a child-centred approach based on texts in language teaching situations that 'immerse students in real communication situations wherever possible' (Froese, 1991). It collates and synthesises the three language arts of speaking and listening, reading and writing and develops them together in situations that are meaningful for the young reader.

In the integrated approach language activities are purposeful and relevant and the learner's previous language experiences, such as sense of story and knowledge of syntax, are used to make sense of the text. Skills teaching, such as phonological awareness and the recognition of letter strings, is incorporated within the context of, and arises from, the text and its meaning and is not taught in separate teaching sessions.

Writing and reading are viewed as reciprocal activities where knowledge of reading and skills can be taught and learned together.

Writing

Chapman (1987, p.3) suggests that 'writing is probably the best way to learn to read'. Such literacy activities include keeping diaries, writing letters and writing stories and can be used to support reading. Such activities can either result from, or lead into, reading a variety of appropriate texts. *The Jolly Postman* (Ahlberg and Ahlberg, 1986) is an excellent book for introducing children to different styles of letter writing as well as reintroducing traditional tales and rhymes. Children's writing using such examples as models can then be valued and used as a reading resource in the classroom. This is not a new idea. Goodacre (1971) suggested that what children think about they can talk about, what they talk about they can write about and what they write they and others can read.

The integrated approach views a reading resource, whether children's or published, as something to be shared and talked about with others, rather than being discarded once finished in the race for progression. Speaking and listening as well as writing become essential elements in the reading process.

Speaking and Listening

Language and language learning are social activities and occur best in situations which encourage discussion and sharing of ideas. Such situations allow children to take risks in their reading and learn from any errors they make in their learning experiences. Children use logic when learning, even though sometimes their logic is inappropriate. Sharing strategies and thinking processes can help children to tune into the appropriate logic for the task in hand.

Communication occurs between teacher and child and between peers. Communication between teacher and child in the reading situation, however, is often restricted to hearing reading. Hearing reading is not sufficient, however, as an aid to progress and understanding. For many children it is a testing situation where they and their abilities are put on public display. If children are to understand what they are reading, which is the major reason for a reading task, they need to be more relaxed. Reading for meaning is not possible when reading aloud focuses on accuracy, as concentration remains at the word level (Smith, 1973), particularly if there has been no opportunity for preparation. Meek (1989) states that what counts as reading in class often becomes a meaningless set of rituals rather than an interaction with the text, especially when the average time spent listening to individual children read is 30 seconds (Southgate, Arnold and Johnson, 1981)!

Children can be helped in comprehending a text through discussion with their peers. Reading for understanding, therefore, needs to be shared.

Comprehension is not always best conducted through questions chosen by the class teacher. The reader should be an active participant in the reading process who is able to interact with the text and who is able to relate knowledge and experience to what is being read. Anderson and Pearson (1984) suggest that comprehending a text is rather like completing a jigsaw where all the information must be used and put into place to make sense of the text.

Not every reader makes the same sense of a text; sharing ideas, therefore, extends children's understanding and response to books whether narrative or information. The primary focus should be on authentic, whole texts (Cairney, 1990) where the purpose for reading and writing is made clear to the pupil and where teachers realise that the meaning is relative to children's experience and is often socially constructed.

The integrated approach to comprehension and understanding, therefore, is concerned less with the retrieval of information that the text offers (although this is also important) and more with the interactive nature of reader and text:

> ...the active encounter of one mind and one imagination with another. (Meek, 1982, pp.10–11)

There is more to reading than skills and understanding. The Bullock Report (DES, 1975) in its definition of reading referred to a *response* to the author's meaning and *English in the National Curriculum* (DFE and WO, 1995, p.13) highlights response to literature in its Programmes of Study.

Reader response

There are few texts that do not demand some kind of response from the reader. Struggling readers who are still reading at the surface level of text, that is, the words rather than their significance and meaning, are limited in the responses that they are able to make. Yet response is a natural consequence of reading (Cairney, 1990) and one which allows children to reflect and to evaluate the experience and effectiveness of a text. It is an active process which makes significance of what children are reading (Hayhoe and Parker, 1990).

The earliest way of enabling children to make responses is through reading stories to them so that they can talk about them. This listening and talking help children to become aware of story book language and meaning. Older, inexperienced readers still need this reaffirmation and consolidation. Listening to stories and talking about them are essential parts of an integrated approach and are necessary to sustain motivation and pleasure.

One of the primary responses to text is the enjoyment a story can give:

> We do not wish to underestimate the straightforward pleasure that reading can afford: an identification of a book with enjoyment and a positive readiness to devote leisure time to reading seems to us wholly desirable outcomes of primary and secondary school experience. (DES and WO, 1989, para. 7.3)

Chambers (1991) suggests that enjoyment is the basis for children to become more thoughtful readers as, once they have enjoyed a book, there is the need to experience the same pleasure, either by re-reading the same book or reading others by the same author and having someone to share them with.

Discussion with peers or with a truly listening and interested adult gives children opportunities to reflect on what they have read. In addition this kind of talk helps to develop skills such as questioning and comparing with other texts which, in turn, enable children to reflect *consciously* about what they have read. In this way children develop and deepen their responses. For many children talking about a book is a crucial way to sort out ideas and events; it allows the abstract to be made concrete as literary experiences are related to personal lives. It is important to capture half formulated ideas that may otherwise have been lost without discussion.

It is equally important to use speaking and listening before reading activities. Discussion about a book's title, its cover or publisher's blurb can build a framework of expectations and predictions that supports struggling readers.

Discussion is only one way in which children can respond to a book. A good book, for example, leaves gaps (Iser, 1978) for readers to fill imaginatively with constructions based on events and characters in the book (what did Buttons do while Cinderella was at the Ball?) or allows questions as to what happens next (what did the Ugly sisters do after the wedding?) or poses problems that need solving (how did Cinderella manage to get home before her sisters when she was on foot and they were in a coach?). All children, including inexperienced readers, should be encouraged to fill gaps and solve problems in pairs or groups and to write their own solutions for others to read. A book can be a starting point for activities. *The Jolly Postman* has already been referred to as a wonderful stimulus for letter writing. It can also be used as a starting point for a whole class activity in researching and reading traditional stories and nursery rhymes and inventing letters for other characters to write and receive. This kind of class activity fully involves the inexperienced reader in reading, writing and talking about texts. Texts can also be responded to by reworking as poems or plays. Dramatic reconstruction of stories need not be written: versions can be read and performed using the text as guidance. It can sometimes be effective to read stories or poems with illustrations removed. Children are then encouraged to engage in the active process of mental imaging and can draw their own illustrations, if necessary. In order to do this they may have to read the text very carefully for descriptions of events and characters to ensure their illustrations are appropriate and effective. In this way re-reading is made purposeful.

Role play is another effective and enjoyable way of re-reading and responding to text where children choose to become a character from a book and defend their actions in response to questions from classmates.

Reflective reading requires re-reading of the text, either to re-explore the enjoyment of the experience or to check for meaning or to get more out of the story. Bloom, Martin and Walters (1988) refer to this process as readerly behaviour. In this way children are able to hear and value other people's interpretations of a text and are able to explore a text more fully. Dombey (1992) maintains that re-reading is important for the understanding of the narrative as a whole. Many of us, having finished a book, realise that we have missed items in our reading. Similarly, re-reading enables inexperienced readers to find 'missing' items and to rediscover with pleasure that which they already knew.

In order for readers to be able to reflect they need texts which give them opportunities to do so. Some reading scheme books, however, seem not to be designed for re-reading for pleasure. Books need to be chosen carefully. Squire (1990) stresses the need for quality literature if children are to be able to respond fully to the text. He maintains that the quality of the literature can affect the quality of response, that high quality and genuine literature evoke 'richer and more meaningful responses' (p.13). Martin (1993) refers to the 'powerful reading contexts' (p.26) of stories and poems. He maintains that:

> Most powerful meanings occur when readers interact with imaginative literature and to be affected by a story or poem is something every child needs to experience. (p.31)

The young reader who is still developing independent strategies needs this experience above all else.

Choice of reading material

Effective response, involving both thinking and feeling, is difficult to develop from restricted texts that have little substance or where meaning

14

only exists at the sentence level. It is important for readers still developing their confidence and competence that they have access to entire contexts (Butzow and Butzow, 1988), for example, a picture book or a story, not in a series of simplified sentences which books written specifically for beginning and struggling readers often are.

Making links with children's previous experience enables texts to become more accessible to them. Previous experience includes the stories and rhymes that inexperienced readers have already encountered; they need specific encouragement to build up and draw upon the rhythms of natural language and story patterns and conventions. Children are better supported when they read words that they use and understand and when they encounter syntactic structures with which they are familiar. On the other hand, if children are not encouraged to use their knowledge and experience to relate what they know to the text, the act of reading is made much more difficult than it need be. Some reading schemes, unfortunately, with stereotypical language, do not offer the opportunity to learn an appropriate range of language patterns and vocabulary.

Young readers, who see others around them engaging in reading and writing activities, begin with the expectation that they also will become literate. Children who have found the going difficult still know that books have meaning, though they may not be familiar with the way the book is organised or the way in which its language works. Every text has a discourse structure which readers expect to understand (Smith, 1982). If the structure is not known, then the understanding of the text is made difficult. If the material bears no resemblance to prior knowledge, reading with understanding becomes problematic. If, for example, a text does not have a forward moving narrative but has a text that makes as much sense backwards as it does forwards (Wade, 1990) or is one that contains material that the child has no experience of factually, emotionally or imaginatively, then the text does not support the reader adequately. Many experienced readers cannot read fluently when presented with unfamiliar language structures or disjointed or meaningless texts. Books should provide interest, imagination and a purpose that children respect, recognise and enjoy (Barrett et al., 1989). They should also add to and complement experience:

The acquisition of skills, including the ability to read, becomes devalued when what one has learned to read adds nothing to the importance of one's life. (Bettelheim, 1976, p.4)

Roberts (1989) states that reading scheme books 'give a peculiar notion of what reading and books are about' and that books should:

...make their readers laugh, touch their feelings and clarify situations in a way that reading scheme books never can or at least never do. (p.15)

For a properly integrated approach, therefore, good quality literature which is supportive to all children should be made available. As well as having access to books that support them as they learn reading strategies, inexperienced readers also require texts that are challenging in content. If children only encounter books where the language is pared down to make reading simple for struggling readers, they will never have the opportunity to progress to what others read and enjoy. Inexperienced readers beyond the age of seven should be encouraged to take some responsibility for their own learning and to become independent in using reading strategies; they do, however, need teacher guidance.

Teaching Reading

There have been erroneous and uninformed assumptions that if reading scheme books are not used then there can be no structure to the teaching of reading. Donaldson (1989) refers to the 'minimal teaching movement' which withholds all systematic help when using 'real' books. Phillips (1990) refers to the 'creeping fashion' for real books where children are 'simply expected to pick it (reading) up'. There is no evidence that teachers have ever followed this kind of fashion. What evidence there is shows that at least 95 per cent do use reading schemes as part of their reading policy (DES, 1991). It is a mistake to believe that the only structured approach is one which rigidly follows a single set of published materials. Indeed, this seems more like an abdication of thinking and structure on the part of teachers. Again the evidence shows that most teachers use a variety of materials and that problems occurred in the small minority which confined children's experience to reading schemes (DES, 1991). The consolidation and extension of reading strategies for all children demands a good deal of thought and structure.

To achieve a successful approach for inexperienced readers beyond the age of seven the teacher's approach must be highly structured and must provide systematic guidance, instruction and motivation. The 1990 Curriculum Guidance (DES and WO, 1990) legislates for a specific teaching of literacy skills and teachers are encouraged to guide their pupils:

> ...to use the available cues, such as pictures, context, phonic cues, word shapes and meaning of a passage to decipher new words, be ready to make informed guesses, and to correct themselves in the light of additional information, e.g. by reading ahead or looking back in the text. (p.30, para. 7)

This is very different from simply testing reading by hearing children read from a reading scheme book. Here the emphasis is placed on teaching rather than on testing. Teaching in the integrated approach requires the ability to keep more than one idea in mind at the same time. Reading is, as we said in our first chapter, a complex behaviour.

We have argued in this chapter that children benefit from an integrated approach where they are taught strategies in context. Discussion goes hand in hand with reading a book (Baker, 1984). Crucially it is discussion with an adult that aids the learning process and strengthens the child's understanding, not only of reading strategies, but also of the relationship between the reader and the text. The adult provides guidance through encouraging the inexperienced reader to reflect on what is being read, to re-read when a miscue has occurred, to encourage the solving of problems and to self correct. The adult has an important role in making explicit what strategies work. It is important to point out the range of cues that are available, including context, graphic, phonic and picture cues. In this way adults encourage active engagement of inexperienced readers in the problem solving process and in developing and extending their own learning. This social interaction between inexperienced readers and adult professionals, what Bruner (1986) refers to as 'scaffolding', enables children to learn in a structured way through contexts and routines that become familiar.

One part of structuring an integrated approach is to move systematically between texts that are familiar to inexperienced readers and those which present new learning challenges. Familiar texts consolidate reading strategies and develop confidence. As soon as a child is reading a book fluently there is less need to read it to the teacher; the book can also be shared with a peer. Sessions with the teacher are useful for introducing unfamiliar texts, for demonstrating how particular strategies work effectively and for recording progress. During these sessions the teacher needs to offer positive encouragement and to observe the child's reading behaviour carefully. These observations and records will structure future teaching sessions so that the child is constantly building on achievements.

Direct teaching in a structured, integrated programme focuses on meaning. Children are encouraged to re-read to check if the reading has made sense. They are encouraged to read on to see whether the context will provide a cue. They are also encouraged, where necessary, to deduce the meaning of individual words from their context. This is where children can be encouraged to use their phonic and graphic knowledge. For example, if re-reading or reading ahead has not provided the 'missing' word, they can be encouraged to look at initial letters or letter strings of the word as another cue. If misreading occurs, they can be encouraged to cross-check between more than one cue. Inexperienced readers need to learn how to check information from context against information from word shape, letters, sounds or picture cues, so that the responsibility of solving the reading problem eventually becomes theirs. This structured approach gives readers support, experience and independence and, at the same time, enables progression.

The most important information a teacher has is knowledge of individual children – what strategies they already have mastered and what they are just on the point of learning as well as how much confidence they have. This information will influence teaching decisions. For example, a child may misread 'girl' as 'lady'. This establishes the fact that the child is reading for meaning and with an unconfident, inexperienced reader may be allowed to pass if the aim is to build confidence and observe behaviour. Eventually, in order for the child to progress, attention will have to be focused on words as well as overall meaning. The teacher, rather than correcting the error immediately, or letting it pass, could return to the word once the sense has been completed to point out what the child has read and bring their phonological strategies into play. For example:

You read that as 'lady'. That makes sense but what does 'lady' begin with? Does that word begin with 'l'? What does it begin with? What could the word be?

In this way instruction is given within the context of meaning and emphasis is on strategies that can be used again and again rather than on the isolated practice of traditional skills teaching.

Group reading is also an effective and efficient classroom strategy for working together on a text, discussing ideas, planning activities or sharing reading strategies. Inexperienced readers learn a good deal from their peers and may need to practise in supportive group sessions before they can read the same material independently. Reading enjoyable books together and seeing how others tackle reading can encourage children to take responsibility when they meet a word that they do not know. Responsibility needs to be planned for. For example, it is better to support group reading by encouraging individuals to check by asking 'does this say ....?' rather than 'what does this say?' The former question marks a considerable shift in confidence, responsibility and learning.

Summary

This chapter has presented and discussed the ways in which the integration of speaking, listening and writing contribute to children's progress and response in reading. It has also shown the importance of an appropriate choice of reading material to encourage children's interest and, when readers are inexperienced, a range of texts that are supportive in terms of content and language structure. Teaching strategies, designed to help the inexperienced reader to progress to independence, have also been described. It has been shown that these strategies are best taught within an integrated context and with suitable texts, a different approach from that of the traditional help given to inexperienced readers. The rest of this book is devoted to exploring shifts in progress. The following chapters describe our research conducted in the West Midlands with groups of children that schools described as struggling readers. We investigated differences in the rate of progress between groups of inexperienced readers taught in the traditional, schematic way and groups who were taught by the integrated approach described in this chapter. The study lasted for a period of 15 months and followed children from Year 3 to Year 4. We analyse our findings and their implications for teaching. We also describe strategies that are part of an integrated approach and that we found to be successful. First, in the next chapter, we outline how we conducted the study.

CHAPTER THREE
Studying Reading Policies

> When you do research you collect and analyse facts and information and try to gain new knowledge or new understanding.
>
> (Collins Cobuild English Language Dictionary, 1987)

Introduction

It was not our intention to determine whether one approach was better than another in the initial teaching of reading. The children who took part in our study had all experienced at least two years teaching and were still working towards independence. They all had difficulties in reading irrespective of the initial teaching they had received. Our intention was to determine which approach would enable children to make more progress in a number of reading areas, including skills and understanding, over a period of time.

Our specific research aim was to assess the relative effectiveness of two broad approaches to teaching children who are described as experiencing difficulty in learning to read. For convenience we have labelled these approaches (i) schematic and (ii) integrated.

(i) The schematic approach

This approach uses structured reading materials as a major resource. It is based upon behaviourist principles of learning with emphasis on learning skills, such as word recognition and phonics, to mastery. New vocabulary is introduced gradually with many repetitions in order that individual words may be learned. Books are sequenced so that new vocabulary is not introduced until previous vocabulary has been learned. The aim is that eventually children build a sight vocabulary together with word attack skills.

This approach is also widely used in the initial teaching of reading, but has been the traditional approach for children with difficulties in reading.

Specific reading schemes have been written for children with reading difficulties (for example, *Racing to Read*, Tansley and Nicholls, 1962).

(ii) The integrated approach

In this approach readers have an involvement with text and their own learning instead of being passive recipients of skills teaching. The report of the English Working Group (DES and WO, 1989) considered reading *not* as a series of discrete steps linked together (para. 16.9) but as a complex and unitary process. Reading is a 'quest for meaning' (p.40) where the reader should be an active participant. The integrated approach incorporates these principles. Reading is not taught as a series of sub-skills, but holistically in conjunction with the other language skills of speaking, listening and writing, which are regarded as interlocking and mutually supportive. Literature is used as the main resource usually with story as a basis (Bennett, 1985; Wade, 1990). The learning emphasis is upon gaining understanding and meaning from the text through contextual clues and the child's previous knowledge of language (Waterland, 1988; Smith, 1991) as well as through word recognition and analysis skills. Learning is further consolidated through the reader's talking and writing. This approach has not been specifically promoted for children who are having difficulties in reading.

The Schools

We began with a questionnaire to a sample of West Midlands primary schools. Only six out of 46 described features that we have labelled integrated in their policy and practice of helping struggling readers at Key Stage 2. Whatever the mainstream policy of teaching reading, the large majority of schools used behaviourist, structured and schematic teaching and materials for their older, inexperienced readers. The study that we describe takes the six schools with integrated policies and matches them with six others that used schematic methods.

Within each group there was one large school which had a rich diversity of culture and ethnic origin, one school with predominantly professional parents, one school with parents who were mainly unskilled or unemployed and three schools in each group that had a mixture of council and private housing with parents who ranged from semi-skilled to professional workers. There was one church school in each group.

The Children

The children were in the Spring term of Year 3, having had a term to settle with their new teachers. They had been selected by their class teachers as having difficulty in reading before we assessed their capabilities. They were not necessarily children with general, moderate learning difficulties although, as we worked with children in the integrated group, it became clear that many of the children had difficulties that went beyond their reading.

In total, 83 children took part in the study: 41 (19 girls, 22 boys) from schools categorised schematic and 42 (17 girls, 25 boys) in schools categorised integrated. The mean age of each group was identical. During the course of the study the numbers in each group reduced to 39 through moving school or prolonged absence.

We established that the mean reading and comprehension ages for each group were compatible: the schematic group had a reading age of 7 years 4.2 months compared with 7 years 5.8 months for the integrated group; each group had a mean comprehension age of 7 years 1 month. Slight differences in reading age were not statistically significant and were negligible for our purpose which was to measure rates and amounts of progress.

Measuring reading progress

We soon realised that, since the reading process is multi-faceted we would require not one, but a variety of approaches. In order to measure progress with more objectivity we used standardised, quantitative tests, although we were aware of the drawbacks of conducting tests that gave only a Reading Age. Many tests concentrate on word recognition (for example, Burt, 1974) or utilise general knowledge under the guise of comprehension (for example, NFER Reading Test AD, 1970). Comprehension is arguably the most important aspect of reading (Smith, 1982) and can be used in conjunction with the skills of word recognition, phonic cues and the contextual cues of language within the language of the text. One standardised test for both Reading Age and Comprehension Age is the Neale Analysis of Reading Ability (1966 and 1989) which assesses both areas of competence and gives a quantitative measure for both. We therefore designed an experiment with the classic pre-test and post-test with our two groups of children. Statistical analysis would then determine whether one approach or the other produced greater changes in measured reading competence.

There are, of course, drawbacks with any experimental research, particularly in an educational context. Ethically we could not have a proper control group as that would have denied some children receiving any reading tuition. Nor could we account for all of the intervening variables (such as intelligence, levels of motivation, attitudes, parental support, teacher enthusiasm) in research on this scale. We could not avoid interactions between ourselves and the children or between ourselves and their class teachers. These factors form some of the irrelevant but influential variables which can influence an experimental design's objectivity. However, it is our view that no educational research is entirely objective.

Further, an awareness of drawbacks lessens their effect. We had two groups of readers matched for chronological age, reading and comprehension ages and distribution of gender and background; in this way we had equated the groups as closely as was possible.

Nevertheless we were still aware that Reading Age and Comprehension Age results, no matter how significant, were only part of the complex picture of reading. In order to investigate more thoroughly, we decided to use multiple and contrasting methods, agreeing with Cohen and Manion (1989) that these would obtain a more confident and truer representation.

Our investigation, therefore, was both experimental and a case study. A case study is more descriptive and evaluative (Merriam, 1988) than objectively measurable; however, case studies can establish motivation and causation in specific contexts. There was a need to know, for example, why certain occurrences had taken place, why one group had made more progress than another. Our case study of interaction between reading and its context was likely to give us more insight into the teaching and learning processes of reading. Also, the information gathered would be more likely to have relevance and implications for teachers and students. Stake (1981) suggests that knowledge gained from case study is:

- More concrete because it interacts with our experience. All primary school teachers, for example, have experience of children who have difficulties in reading.

- More contextual because experience is rooted in context. Teachers are aware of the problems such children face in the classroom.

- More developed by reader interpretation as readers bring to a case study their own experience and understanding. Teachers can make links between their own pupils and teaching methods with those suggested in this book.

- Based on a reference population determined by the reader. Most teachers would have a specific population of children with difficulties in reading in mind and could generalise and speculate about the results that we give here.

There are, of course, disadvantages with case study research. Crossley and Vulliamy (1984) mention lack of rigour in case study methods as a basis for accusations of bias and lack of generalisability. Triangulation, however, is one technique which can enhance reliability and validity. We concentrated on Theoretical, Time and Methodological Triangulation.

Theoretical Triangulation attempts to provide a more balanced perspective by drawing upon more than one theoretical viewpoint rather than working from a single perspective which can lead to distortion of data. Our research, both in its design and in the analysis of the data, takes into consideration the theoretical implications of the two approaches to reading.

Time Triangulation overcomes the difficulties of taking one set of measurements at one point in time which ignores variables such as development and change in the children. Two points of measurement, pre and post the research period, enabled us to make comparisons between groups at two points in time and measured the progress of the two groups.

Methodological Triangulation is the use of different types of data collection. We decided to use standardised tests of reading and comprehension, but also intonation analysis, attitude tests and interviews plus an assessment of difficulty of self chosen texts and children's accuracy and fluency of reading their chosen texts.

Research strategies

(i) Reading Test

We chose the Neale Analysis of Reading Test for a number of reasons:

- Its use of continuous prose: a simple narrative would enable children to read language in a meaningful context rather than reading words in isolation or in a series of unrelated sentences.

- Its use of illustrations: the illustrations, together with the narrative, would enable the reader to formulate a context and give cues to the reading. They also make the text look more like a book than the majority of other tests. In addition they gave children the opportunity to talk to us and made assessment sessions more relaxed than they might otherwise have been.

● Its use of comprehension questions: although many of the questions were at the literal or reorganisation level, they did allow us to make an assessment of whether the children were reading at a mechanical level or with some understanding.

The concepts of Reading Age and Comprehension Age have been questioned but the function of our test was to measure the amount of progress between the groups, not to assess children's reading and comprehension ages at one moment in time.

We used three types of statistical measurement:

● one way Analysis of Variance, repeated measures;

● Newman-Keuls post hoc test;

● t-test.

These compute the levels of significance of average scores for the group. More detail is given in Chapter 4.

(ii) Intonation Analysis

Intonation in speech is a conscious choice made by the reader. It varies with context and gives additional emphasis and meaning to what is being said. Choice of intonation is as important in reading aloud as it is in speech. It gives meaning to the printed word and communicates to the listener the reader's understanding of the writer's intent. Choice and use of intonation can indicate, therefore, to what extent the reader has internalised the meaning of the written text. A newscaster chooses intonation suitable for giving information, while a story reader needs to command the attention of the audience and invite the listener to share emotions engendered by the story such as suspense and surprise. We predicted therefore, that children who understood the stories they were reading would use intonation appropriate for storytelling.

It would have been easy to make a subjective analysis of the children's intonation competence, but this subjectivity could have led to a bias in our reporting. We therefore decided to use a more objective analysis of intonation. We chose the analysis suggested by Brazil, Coulthard and Jones (1980) as it focuses on contextual meaning rather than remaining at the level of grammar. A brief explanation of the processes of analysis is given in Chapter 4.

(iii) Attitude Test

Attitudes are largely determined by experience, interaction and environment. Attitudes towards school subjects, for example, can be determined by good or poor teaching, adult interest and teaching methods. Such attitudes may then affect school learning. Children's attitudes to reading can affect whether or not they view reading as important to them, whether or not they are motivated to read to learn or progress in their reading, whether or not they choose to read books. Assessment of attitudes, however, is difficult. It is possible to observe children's behaviour, but behaviour does not always correlate with attitudes. In the classroom, conformity to what children know is acceptable to adults can often mask attitudes to reading. Children may go through the motions of reading, but without interest or pleasure; or they may pay lip service to the benefits of reading without putting in the necessary effort to reap that benefit.

We decided that we would obtain a fuller assessment of children's attitudes if we linked some observation with an attitude test (see Chapter 6). We based our attitude test on a Likert type scale. This consists of an equal number of favourable and unfavourable statements, in our case, towards reading. We used 12 items which, it is suggested (for example, Verma and Beard, 1981), give an estimate of a wide range of attitudes. We ensured that they were clear, simple and unambiguous by running a pilot test with a group of children and taking account of comments and suggestions they made.

Each statement is followed by a rating scale. The usual rating scale consists of five points but we took into account the age of the children, the length of time for the whole assessment and the boredom factor and cut it to three points. Each statement is either positive or negative towards reading and is scored differently to reflect the degree of positiveness, for example:

Reading is interesting: Agree – 3   Not sure – 2   Disagree – 1
Reading is boring: Agree – 1   Not sure – 2   Disagree – 3

There are problems in validating attitude tests and in estimating their reliability. Our view was that the attitude test that we administered would at best give an indication of attitudes the children were willing to reveal or possibly what they thought we wanted to hear. In order to double check the attitude test results we therefore decided to conduct a follow-up interview where we raised similar issues.

(iv) Interview

Interview is widely regarded as an essential source of evidence in case studies (Yin, 1989). We certainly considered it essential in our work both to pursue topics in depth and to establish a rapport between the children and ourselves. Interview as a technique has its own drawbacks of subjectivity, bias and eagerness to please.

Adults are inevitably in an authority relationship with children and thus we tried to be sensitive to their needs and misgivings. We followed the advice of Powney and Watts (1987) who suggest that interviews with children:

> ...should follow the courtesies of adult interviews. These include the careful attention to explanation and listening to responses...and possible checking back with the children that the interviewer has got it right. (Powney and Watts, 1987, p.48)

We ensured that children were at ease and treated them sympathetically and politely in order that they were confident with us. We worked in surroundings familiar to the children and used a tape recorder rather than taking notes. Children quickly become accustomed to a tape recorder; once in use it is less obtrusive than taking notes. It also ensures that everything is recorded rather than just that which researchers want to hear!

We used a semi-structured interview which had set areas of questions (see Appendix 1), but which allowed children to explore the topics if they wished.

Part of the interview related to children's responses about the book they were currently reading. We wished to analyse these responses as objectively as possible and so adapted a model of reader response to suit the age of the children.

(v) Reader response

There is no standardised procedure for the analysis of children's responses to fiction; neither is there any globally accepted developmental theory which charts children's progress from simple responses to fiction to increasingly complex and sophisticated levels of response. There are models of response, however, (for example, Thomson, 1987) which have been developed as a result of categorising responses made by large numbers of children from a range of ages. We chose the model provided by Protherough (1983) as a basis for the analysis of children's responses to fiction and made adaptations to suit the circumstances and the age range of the children in our research. Chapter 6 describes the model and the adaptations that we made.

How we proceeded

Our initial testing was done over a five week period in the twelve schools. Each session began with a discussion with the head teacher in which we reiterated the purpose of the investigation, that is to assess the progress made in reading. The school was assured of anonymity. We were then introduced to the children. Our concern was that they might be shy, or even upset, in the presence of a stranger. We were therefore keen that the proceedings should be as informal as possible. The children started off as a group so that they could gain confidence and support from each other. We explained that we were trying to find out about reading, for example, what kind of reading children liked, and that they had been chosen to help. They were told that they would have some reading to do and that they would answer questions in an interview. At this point we asked the children if they wanted to help. We emphasised that if they did not want to help it did not matter and, perhaps more importantly to them, that they would not get into trouble for refusing. Everyone agreed to take part.

We started with the first questions of the interview as these could be completed as a group activity. The group drew 'smiley faces' in response to questions about their favourite activity and a 'really miserable face' for something they hated doing and then an 'I don't mind face'. These activities gave the children opportunity to talk and demonstrated their understanding of which face represented which mood. We then asked them to draw the appropriate face for the question related to reading. The children appeared relaxed, to be having fun and seemed to find the activity meaningful. The remaining interview questions were left for later responses while the attitude tests were completed.

The attitude tests were also completed as a group. In retrospect it may have been better to have conducted them in pairs as most children spent a long time debating the questions. However, we thought it more important that they should be relaxed and motivated.

When the attitude test had been completed, we told the children that they would be in pairs for the next activity and that we would send for them when necessary. The next activity was the reading test. We told the children they could choose a friend to be with them during the reading, as we realised the importance of an appropriate and non-threatening context (Labov, 1970). The Neale Analysis of Reading Ability has parallel tests which did not give the non-participants an unfair advantage when it was their turn. We emphasised the importance of not giving any words during their friend's reading or answering the questions in the comprehension test. We did, however, talk about the text afterwards.

It was essential that the children should not feel under any stress or feel in any way that they had failed. Accordingly it was emphasised that the reading was difficult to do and that they should not be worried if there were any words they could not read; they should simply try to do their best. Before they started to read we told them again how important their contribution was to our research.

We sat between the two children and placed the book in front of the reader in an attempt to make the situation as close to a normal reading situation as possible to enable them to read to the best of their ability, rather than thinking they were just being tested.

The test was conducted to the standardised format. We then encouraged and praised each child after every story, particularly if they had found it difficult. We accepted all answers to the questions verbally, but scored them according to the prescribed criteria.

After the tests had been completed for both children, we returned to the interview questions and a more informal situation. The questions were asked of both children at the same session and we added a child's name at the end of each question, ensuring that each had an equal number of first goes at answering them. The interview concluded the initial assessment and we thanked the children for having taken part and asked if they would take part if they were needed again. All children replied 'yes'.

The final assessment, at the end of the research period, followed the same procedure. Many of the children remembered the first assessment, particularly when the 'smiley faces' activity was reintroduced. There was one addition to the final assessment for both groups. We wrote to schools about the final assessment, requesting that children should bring a favourite book with them to the session.

After children had finished their reading test, we asked them to choose part of their book and read it aloud. They were given as much time as they needed to practise. We tape recorded their reading and these recordings formed the basis for our intonation analysis, an analysis of the level of difficulty of the book and a measure of children's fluency in reading. We then asked each child questions about their book which allowed analysis of levels of reader response. Finally we completed the interview questions in the same way that we had done in the initial assessment session.

The fifteen month period between the initial and final assessment formed the experimental span of our research. During this time the Integrated Groups had seven brief visits for work on integrated language activities. This was, in some cases, an extension of work they were doing in their classrooms. Inevitably there were differences between the 'integrated' schools in their approaches and we needed to ensure their pupils actually engaged in holistic language activities focused on reading. These integrated language activities are briefly described here but are presented and discussed in detail together with implications for classroom teaching in Chapter 8.

Summary

This chapter has briefly described the schools in our sample, the two approaches to the teaching of reading used by the schools and the children who took part in our study. It also outlines reasons for choice of data collection, the types of assessments we used and the procedures we adopted. The following chapters present the results of our study.

CHAPTER FOUR
Progress in Reading and Comprehension

I can correct myself if I get some of the words wrong/but sometimes other people/they tell me what the words are and they help me and ask me things about the book/do you like it/what's it about.

Angelina (age 8)

Introduction

In this chapter and those that follow we discuss the findings of our study and offer implications for teaching inexperienced readers to develop the strategies that they need for independent reading. We focus on fluency in reading in Chapter 5, attitudes and response to literature in Chapter 6 and the results of interviews with the children in Chapter 7.

In this chapter we analyse and discuss results of standardised tests of reading and comprehension. In addition we present results of our intonation analysis of reading aloud which also assessed comprehension.

The children in the Integrated Groups, it will be remembered, had an approach to reading which incorporated Speaking and Listening, Writing and Reading activities and which used freely chosen literature for reading texts. The Schematic Groups, on the other hand, received a structured programme of reading schemes and specific skills teaching.

Summary of Procedures

Before presenting the results of reading and comprehension age gains it will be useful to recapitulate briefly how we obtained them.

The investigation was conducted over a 15 month period. There were 39 children from six schools in each group for the final assessment. All of the children had been selected by their school as having difficulties in reading. They were all in the Spring term of Year 3 at the initial assessment and in the Summer term of Year 4 for our final assessments.

The selected test for reading and comprehension age was the Neale Test of Reading Ability (1966). Although the reading and comprehension tests were conducted individually the use of parallel tests enabled each child to have a friend present during their own session and to remain during their friend's assessment. This allowed a more informal atmosphere to prevail and there were opportunities for natural, social talk between the children and the interviewer. This procedure was not likely to have an influence on results except that children who are relaxed are more likely to perform at their optimum level (Zigler, Abelson and Seitz, 1973; Cazden, 1979).

The initial assessments for the whole sample were conducted within a three week period in March of the first year. Thereafter the children in the experimental group received seven sessions of integrated language activities, in addition to their usual class integrated language activities, between April of that year and April of the next. The second and final assessment for the whole sample took place in a two week period in June/July at the end of the second year.

The results of both tests were subjected to statistical analysis to determine whether any differences in progress between the groups was significant. These were:

- one way Analysis of Variance, repeated measures;

- Newman-Keuls post hoc test;

- t-test.

The Analysis of Variance determines any levels of statistical significance between two scores. The Newman-Keuls post hoc test determines the point at which the significant difference lies between the groups. In other words, is the difference between the groups only significant after the period of intervention or is there a significant difference before the intervention? A t-test determines more specifically where the difference, if any, lies in the numerical change between the initial and final scores:

- between the schematic and integrated groups;

- between boys in the schematic and integrated groups;

- between girls in the schematic and integrated groups.

Numerical gains, however, do not measure *rate* of progress. We therefore conducted a t-test analysis on the *percentage change* scores of the two groups to determine any significant differences in the rates of progress between them. The following example illustrates why this was necessary: a gain of 50 points from 50 to 100 is equal to a numerical gain from 100 to 150. However, the percentage gain for the first is 100 per cent but for the second only 50 per cent – a considerable difference.

We conducted the intonation analysis of the children's reading after the second assessment session. Children read from a self selected, prepared text and the reading was tape recorded. We subjected these tape recordings to careful scrutiny and their analysis is presented towards the end of this chapter. First, however, we offer the results of the reading age assessments.

Reading Age results

The reading age results presented in this section represent the gain in months made by the two groups during the period of research. They are, therefore, progress scores rather than a simple measure of reading age.

At the beginning of our study the mean reading age for both groups was compatible, with an approximate difference of only 1.5 months. At the end of the study period the mean gain for the Schematic Groups was 12 months and for the Integrated Groups 16.54 months. In other words, children in Integrated Groups had made an average of four and a half months more progress than those in Schematic Groups. We subjected these results to tests for significance and found that the means differed significantly at the 1% level. In other words it is extremely unlikely that the results we obtained could have happened by chance. The Newman-Keuls post hoc statistical test confirmed that the slight difference between reading ages at the start of the study was insignificant. The only significant difference lay in the final scores.

We subjected our results to a statistical t-test in order to gain more information about subgroups of boys and girls. The t-test also confirmed that the groups' mean numerical scores were significant, but it also revealed interesting findings about performances by boys and girls. Boys in the Schematic Groups progressed by 11.86 months and in the Integrated Groups 16.67 months; a difference of 4.81 months. Girls in the Schematic Groups progressed by 12.06 months and in the Integrated Groups by 15.20 months; a difference of 3.14 months. Thus, on the whole, boys in our Integrated Groups made more progress than girls and their results were at a higher level of significance (1% compared with 5%). This is an encouraging finding, since the majority of pupils still encountering difficulties in reading at seven years of age and older are boys. However, our results show that both boys and girls benefit from an integrated, holistic approach to reading. The t-test analysis of percentage gain scores confirmed the levels of significance, reaffirming that the results were most unlikely to have occurred by chance.

So far, results have been encouraging and have indicated more achievement for those pupils in the Integrated Groups. However, it is important to remember that we have only assessed one dimension of the complex behaviour of reading. The ability to decode print with accuracy is not the only indicator of reading competence. There are readers who, for one reason or another, have learned to sound out words, but have very little idea what they mean. It is important, therefore, to find out how far developing readers are, in fact, reading with understanding. The results of the Comprehension tests provided opportunity to assess how our groups compared in this respect.

Comprehension Age results

As with the Reading Age scores that we have just discussed, Comprehension Age scores that follow are progress scores, that is, they record the number of months gained during the investigation period. In this way we can find out the difference in progress between the two groups.

Both groups made gains in their scores for Comprehension Age during the period of the investigation. The Schematic Groups made 14 months progress, but the Integrated Groups improved their original scores by 22.80 months. These are mean scores and they differ significantly at the 0.1% level. This means that the results were extremely unlikely to have occurred by chance. The difference of 8.80 months in favour of the Integrated Groups is an important finding, since comprehension is an essential part of reading competence. Not only is understanding crucial for gaining information from texts, but also the reader who has struggled, but still does not understand, is more likely to lose motivation. The Integrated Approach shows potential for developing comprehension in these inexperienced readers who so far have struggled to reach independence. The Newman-Keuls post hoc statistical test confirmed that the slight difference between comprehension ages at the start of the study was insignificant. The only significant difference lay in the final scores.

We again subjected our results to a statistical t-test in order to gain more information about subgroups of boys and girls. This t-test also confirmed that the groups' mean numerical scores were significant and revealed more interesting findings about performances by boys and girls. Boys in the Schematic Groups progressed by 14.32 months and in the Integrated Groups 24 months; a difference of 9.68 months. Girls in the Schematic Groups progressed by 13.59 months and in the Integrated Groups by 19.27 months; a difference of 5.68 months. Thus, on the whole, boys in our Integrated Groups made even more progress than girls and their results were at a higher level of significance (0.1% compared with 10%).

Again these results are encouraging for both boys and girls and they indicate the potential of holistic approaches in establishing more progress in reading comprehension.

The t-test for percentage gain scores revealed the same levels of significance, reaffirming that increases in comprehension ages were highly unlikely to have occurred by chance.

Quantitative Results: Discussion

These quantitative results so far lead to the conclusion that the integrated approach to the teaching of reading for this sample of inexperienced readers has led to significantly greater gains in reading and comprehension age over a 15 month period. Although our results are significant both for total groups and single sex groups the greater significance lies in the boys' results. If, as it is suggested, boys lose interest in reading more quickly (for example, Whitehead et al., 1977), then an approach which enables them to progress at a greater rate than the traditional methods used for children with reading difficulties has to be beneficial. Fluent readers are more likely to have positive attitudes to reading and are therefore likely to read more and progress more, thus reversing the downward spiral of reading difficulty.

Reading Age tests evaluate the skill levels of readers as they decode text. However, the integrated approach, while it facilitates development of skills, does so in the context of reading and writing whole texts. This approach, where skills are taught as they are needed, has enabled children in this study to make more gains in skills than their counterparts who have specific skills teaching. The greater gains, however, are those for comprehension age. The integrated approach, with its emphasis on choice of literature, opportunity for discussion of books either with peers or tutors and a context where the language arts are supportive, facilitates significantly greater gains in understanding.

Although the results of the standardised tests are positive and encouraging, it has to be recognised that such tests on their own cannot give the whole picture of children's reading. Accuracy and fluency, as we have already suggested, do not necessarily denote understanding of a text. It is easy to sound fluent when reading inaccurately (what Southgate, Arnold and Johnson, 1981, refer to as false fluency) and reading word for word from a text, however accurate, can be as meaningless to the reader as reading a list of unrelated words. Expressive oral reading is only possible when the text is fully understood and the reader has sufficient skill to look ahead of the text (Southgate, Arnold and Johnson, p.288). The expression children use in reading aloud, their intonation choice, is therefore a useful guide to their understanding of reading. In order to obtain a valid sample of intonation patterns children need to be assessed when reading texts that they are familiar with and ones they have chosen to read.

It is often easy for a listener to make assumptions as to whether or not the reader is reading with appropriate expression. These assessments, however, are subjective and are therefore not necessarily accurate. For example, children who are reading in a second language often imitate intonation patterns (as infants do in their mother tongue) and this can give a false picture of their actual understanding. What matters is the appropriateness of intonation in relation to text and in order to assess this aspect a more objective analysis of intonation while reading aloud is required. The next section outlines as simply as possible the features of the system of discourse analysis that we considered most effective for our purposes. For a fuller explanation the reader is referred to the original source (Brazil, Coulthard and Jones, 1980).

Intonation

Appropriate expression and intonation are included in criteria which judge a competent reader (for example, Attainment Target 2, Levels 3 and 4, National Curriculum for English, DES and WO, 1990).

Reading of a story aloud demands shared involvement and understanding between reader and listener. The reader makes the reading interesting by dramatising the text through the use of expression and intonation. The choice of intonation, the way the speech rises and falls, adds a great deal to the communicative value of what is being read. A story read in monotone is very boring to a listener. Good story readers and tellers make full use of their voices (Berry, 1975) and make consciously appropriate intonation choices. Such choices show that the reader is aware of what is going on in the text and is making decisions to communicate meaning as the reading progresses.

There are, therefore, two levels at which intonation can be judged: firstly a subjective assessment of intonation as to whether it is appropriate; or, secondly, an objective approach which analyses particular stresses, tones and pitch appropriate for (in this study) the reading of stories. We chose the latter to avoid error and bias as far as possible.

Before the final assessment sessions we concentrated on children in the Schematic Groups. They had had little contact with us during the study period and to compensate for this we devised informal sessions for them alone. Children in the Integrated Groups had had contact with us in the specific language activity sessions. All children came to the final

36

assessment session in pairs. They had been asked to bring a book with which they were familiar and which they would like to read to others. All of them, therefore, read from a book that they had chosen themselves and one which we assumed that they enjoyed reading. We endeavoured to make the session as interesting and relaxed as possible for the children, but we also made it purposeful. We told the children that their reading was for other children to listen to on tape. We wanted the children to have a clear sense of audience so that they would make their reading interesting. As well as this focus on audience we made further attempts to make the reading as little like a test as possible. They were given time to choose the pages that they wanted to read and were given as much practice time as they wanted. They were also given opportunities to practise with the cassette recorder and were given the choice to record their own reading rather than one of us doing it for them. The majority opted for this responsibility. We also allowed them to listen to their recordings afterwards, if they wished. Most of them did.

Two judges, familiar with the intonation analysis chosen for this study, listened to all of the recordings and made analyses of the intonation patterns used by each child. A third judge then independently verified the results. We now give a brief outline of the system of analysis that we used.

Fundamental to the analysis of intonation are the concepts of **Tone Unit**, **Tone** and **Key**. Speech can be analysed into a series of units of intonation either rising or falling in tone. These units are called **Tone Units**. Recordings are made of choice of **Tone** and **Key** that readers make within tone units.

(a) Tone

A sentence such as 'It's looking at us' can be given different meanings depending on the rise and fall in speech. In the examples that follow, readers are invited to experiment by reading the sentence appropriately for each suggested meaning. The direction of the rise and fall of speech is indicated by the **Tone**. There are five tones described by Brazil et al.:

(i) referring (**r** a tone that falls and then rises) – indicating reference to shared information. For example, in answer to the question, 'What is it doing'?

// r it's LOOKing at us // (to convey: 'as it usually does')

A story is a sharing event and often some, or most, of the information in the story will be known to listener and reader. A referring tone is used for those parts it is assumed that the reader already knows.

(ii) intensified referring (**r+** a rising tone) – indicating dominance and establishing the right to continue speaking;

> // r+   it's LOOKing at us // (to convey: 'I do wish you'd stop asking the same question')

It is an intonation device used particularly by teachers and storytellers! In story reading it is used appropriately to create suspense and to hold attention.

(iii) proclaiming (**p** a falling tone) – indicating that the information is not a shared knowledge:

> // p   it's LOOKing at us // (to convey: 'I assume you have no idea of what the creature's habits are or what it can do')

The appropriate use for a proclaiming tone is for information that the reader is unlikely to share already. It is also appropriate when a conjunction is emphasised which suggests that the following information is important to the listener and that the reader wants attention:

> // p   AND //

(iv) intensified proclaiming (**p+** a tone that rises and then falls) – indicating that the information is new to both speaker and listener, a surprise to both:

> // p+   it's LOOKing at us // (and I'm as surprised as you are)

(v) neutral (**o** a level tone) – indicating a preoccupation with the language itself rather than with the meaning and the interaction. It is associated with incompleteness of discourse, or quoting:

> (it says here) // o   it's LOOKing at us //

or the chanting of prayers in church or tables in school. When children are tested on their reading, or are struggling to read difficult text, they sometimes use a neutral tone because they are concentrating on decoding rather than meaning.

(b) Key

Whereas tone refers to movement of pitch, key is used to describe pitch level.

The three **Keys** (high, mid and low) denote choices made by the reader. These do not have an absolute value but have relative value in relation to preceding and following syllables.

(i) *high key* – marking information as contrastive:

```
high                                    FISH
mid // p   he eats MEAT // r   not          //
low
```

In story reading the contrastive high key can be used as a device to indicate surprise or an unexpected event to the listener.

(ii) *mid key* – a mid point from which high and low key can be marked.

(iii) *low key* – marking information as equivalent, where one phrase is understood to have the same meaning as the one preceding it:

```
high
mid // r   my CAT //                //
low                     r   JAMES
```

In a shared understanding the listener is already aware that James and the cat are the same animal.

The use of a low key can also indicate termination of an utterance, a signal that the speaker has finished that part of the discourse:

```
high
mid // r   and THEN he went //           //
low                          p   HOME
```

The choice of high or low key is made by readers for listeners appropriate to meaning and context and therefore we can associate such appropriate choices with an understanding of what is being read.

The expectation that we have of readers is that, if they understand a passage and are able to take into account the needs of the listener, then they will make appropriate choices between 'r' and 'p' tones with some use made of the 'r+' tone and with a variety of key.

As a result of our intonation analyses, each child's reading aloud was placed into one of the following categories: (a) appropriate, (b) inconsistent or (c) inappropriate.

(a) *Appropriate*

This included appropriate use of:

- the referring tones ('r' and 'r+') to indicate a shared experience between the reader and the listener with the reader being dominant in the discourse (for example, 'Once upon a time...'). In other words the reader did not provide the listener with opportunities to interrupt;

- the proclaiming tone, ('p') to impart information which is new to the reader. For example, Joseph read:

```
high                      REAL
mid //  p   THIS is about        witches  //
low
```

in the proclaiming tone, which suggests to the reader that, even though the story is about witches, it is *not* a fairy tale;

- variety of key (in the example above, the fact that the witches are real is a surprise for the listener).

(b) *Inappropriate*

Inappropriate use of intonation in reading stories aloud included:

- predominant use of the 'p' tone, not used to impart information but used indiscriminately;

- predominant use of the 'o' (neutral) tone;

- little or no variety of key.

(c) *Inconsistent*

This category was reserved for those children who some times used appropriate intonation in their reading, but at other times showed little awareness of appropriate tone or key.

The length of readings varied from child to child, depending on the texts they chose, but in all cases it was possible to assign readings to one of the above categories (a, b or c), since judgements and comparisons were made, not on length, but on how tone and key were used. Because of a few recording failures/erasures or inaudibility, not every child was recorded correctly. Nonetheless 36 transcripts from the Integrated Groups and 35 from the Schematic Groups were analysed – a very satisfactory sample. Results are summarised in Table 4.1.

Table 4.1: Categories of intonation when reading aloud

Category	Group	
	Integrated	Schematic
Appropriate	18	2
Inappropriate	4	20
Inconsistent	14	13
Total	36	35

Table 4.1 shows that the Integrated Groups used far more appropriate intonation than the Schematic Groups in their reading. In fact, only two of the Schematic Group used appropriate intonation consistently, whereas 18 of the Integrated Group did. Thirteen children in the Schematic Groups used an appropriate intonation at some times in their reading. The most interesting result was that 20 of the Schematic Group used an inappropriate intonation for the majority of their reading with an overdependency on a proclaiming or neutral tone. This phenomenon is sometimes evident in young children who are being taught their sight vocabulary when they are described as 'barking at print'.

The conclusion follows, therefore, that most of the Schematic Group did not appear to understand what they were reading, even when they had chosen the book themselves and had had the opportunity to practise their reading. Thirty of the Schematic Group brought their scheme reading book to the assessment session, so it may have been that their choice was a restricted one. Restricted choice, therefore, would seem to have an influence both on reading intonation and understanding of the text.

Reference has been made to the lack of meaningful text in some scheme books (Moon, 1988; Meek, 1988; Wade, 1990). If the text is not meaningful then possibilities for reading with meaning are seriously curtailed. However, if opportunities are not given for meaningful reading then the first priority for successful reading, reading and wanting to read (Southgate, 1973), cannot be met.

A detailed examination of two transcripts (see Appendix 2) will show the interested reader how intonation conveys meaning from text. Two children from our samples are reading from books judged by independent judges to be 'average' for the age of the reader (8+ years). Joseph, from the Integrated Groups, is reading from *The Witches* by Roald Dahl and is accurate and fluent in his reading (see Chapter 8). Similarly, Brendan, from the Schematic Groups is also accurate and fluent in his reading and he is reading *Brave as a Lion*, an extract from *The Wizard of Oz* (Longman Reading World series). Without an intonation analysis, both readers might be simply judged as fluent and accurate.

The transcripts show that Joseph and Brendan use a greater proportion of 'p' than 'r' and 'r+' tones. Joseph, however, uses 'r' or 'r+' proportionally twice as often (15 in 41 tone units) than Brendan (7 in 42 tone units). However, numerical count by itself is not sufficient indication of appropriate use.

Both Joseph and Brendan introduce their reading with the use of 'r+' which is the conventional tone for introducing a story:

// r+   ONCE upon a <u>TIME</u> //

Joseph continues to make appropriate use of the tone, for example, the shared understanding that witches wear silly black hats and ride broomsticks.

His use of the 'p' tone imparts information that is new to the reader and that the listener needs to have this important, new information:

// p   the MOST important THING you should <u>KNOW</u> //

and he continues to use the 'p' tone to inform the listener that real witches are ordinary women who lead ordinary lives, which is why they are so dangerous. For readers of traditional stories this is not shared information and indicates Joseph's sensitivity to the meaning of the text and the needs of his listener.

Brendan's use of the 'p' tone, however, is not always used to give new information:

// o   a <u>GREAT</u> // p   <u>LION</u> // p   <u>POUNCED</u> //

// p   <u>IN</u>to // p   the <u>ROAD</u> // p   with <u>ONE</u> //

// p   <u>BLOW</u> //

The tone units carry no information but tend to be one or two words that do not carry the meaning forward and reveal no apparent choice of intonation being made to impart meaning to the reading.

Brendan has very little change in key in his reading which could, for example, denote surprise or indicate a sequence closure. Joseph, on the other hand, makes frequent key changes:

high   <u>REAL</u>

mid // p   THIS is about   witches //

low

high   ORdinary

mid // they LIVE in   <u>HOUS</u>es //

low

The use of the high key denotes contrast or indicates that this information is somewhat unexpected and unusual. The use of a low key:

```
high

mid // p    but THIS // p    is NOT // p    a                    //

low                                              FAIRy tale
```

denotes a sequence closure; Joseph is about to start something new:

```
high                              REAL

mid    // p    THIS is about         WITCHES    //

low
```

Analysis of these readings suggests that Joseph is reading with meaning and understanding, whilst Brendan's reading, though accurate, is inappropriate for a story. It indicates that he is a reader who is concentrating more on accurately decoding the words on the page than he is on his listener or on the meaning of the words he is reading.

Later we discuss the level of demand of the books that children in both groups chose to read aloud to us. At this point, however, it is interesting to note that a breakdown of the difficulty level of the books read with appropriate intonation by 18 children in the Integrated Groups is as follows:

demanding   6
average–demanding 1
average   8
easy   3

It can be seen, therefore, that appropriate intonation was not confined to easy books.

It is highly likely that previous experience of the school context provides the major source of difference between groups. The Integrated Group schools, with their main focus on a holistic policy of language teaching, ensured a wide variety of texts with more freedom for the children to choose, therefore maximising the children's interest in reading. Interactive activities of reading, writing and talking about books help to focus attention onto the meaning of text. If children are encouraged to read to each other for enjoyment rather than as practice for accuracy, they are more likely to choose appropriately varied intonation patterns. The schools which used the schematic approach with their children were more likely to focus on the skills of reading with less focus on sharing reading with others, except, perhaps, for testing accuracy.

We must acknowledge at this point that a focus on intonation as an indicator of understanding necessarily emphasises reading aloud. We must not assume that in reading silently children employ exactly the same processes as when reading aloud. Reading aloud is a skill which some children do not enjoy (Allington, 1983; Findlay, 1986). It is a performance in which some children do better than others. The positive aspect of these findings is that children described as having difficulty with reading can enhance their performance and develop their potential for enjoying books, depending on the approach used.

Summary

This chapter has presented results for Integrated and Schematic Groups of children on measures of Reading Age, Comprehension Age and systematic analysis of reading intonation. Children in Integrated Groups made significantly more progress in Reading Age and in Comprehension Age over a 15 month period, as measured by quantitative, standardised tests. Analysis of their intonation patterns showed that more of the Integrated Groups used appropriate reading intonation than Schematic Group members whose choice of intonation was more likely to be inconsistent or inappropriate. Reading aloud to teachers, when the implicit emphasis is on accuracy, encourages minimal reader involvement with the text and the listener. Reading activities which encourage direct orientation to the listener, such as a prepared reading for a known audience, enhance not only accuracy (which is important), but understanding (which is essential).

CHAPTER FIVE
Difficulty of Text and Fluency of Reading

> I started when I was about seven/and I kind of got really excited that we
> started/like/proper books/not like the cards now/and um like I really started
> enjoying it but/I found it was/like a little bit easier 'cos I could look a little
> bit bit ahead and try to figure it out/anyway so it was a lot easier.
>
> Peter (age 13)

Introduction

The intonation analysis that we described in the previous chapter was
made from tape recordings of children reading from self chosen books.
These recordings also provided an opportunity for independent judges to
assess, not only accuracy, but also the fluency of their readings.
Judgements were also made about the complexity of text chosen.

At this point, it is useful to remember that, if children are reasonably
relaxed, they are more likely to read fluently and accurately. As stated in
the previous chapter, we made these reading assessment sessions as little
like a test as possible. The children were assessed in pairs, they had the
notion of an audience apart from ourselves to read to, they had time to
rehearse their reading and they were reading from a book that they had
chosen. They later had the chance to listen to their recordings.

Complexity of Text

As there was such a wide range of texts chosen by the children,
complexity and difficulty of texts varied within and between groups.
Complexity and difficulty significantly influence the accuracy and
fluency of reading. A child may read one text at frustration level and
another, easier one, at an independent level of reading. We wanted to
ascertain at which level of complexity of text the children chose to read,
since fair comparisons between groups on accuracy and fluency could not
be made without also determining whether the chosen texts were easy or
demanding.

Assessments of texts were not made by formulaic devices, such as readability measures, since these rely on mechanistic syllable count or sentence length (Harrison, 1979) and do not take into account the complexity of spelling, sentence construction or the ideas contained in the text which readers need to understand if they are to read with expression and meaning. A more sensitive, if less objective, measure was therefore taken. We recorded each book title as the children read and also noted this for later checking.

First, we made a provisional assessment of the appropriate level of the chosen text for the 8–9 year age range. At a later date two judges, both experienced in the teaching of reading and knowledgeable about children's literature, made more precise assessments of the level of difficulty from listening to the taped responses and from their knowledge of the actual books used. In most cases chosen texts were already known to the judges whether as free standing books or those from reading schemes. Their classifications took account of other assessments such as the *Kaleidoscope* guide (Moon, *Individualised Reading*, revised annually) and also the specific level of difficulty of the section of the book being read. Vocabulary, sentence construction and complexity of ideas within the text were taken into consideration.

As a result of these assessments texts were assigned to one of the following categories:

(a) demanding
(b) average–demanding
(c) average
(d) average–easy
(e) easy.

An example of a demanding text, because of its construction and complex ideas, was *The Walrus and the Carpenter* from *Through the Looking Glass* by Lewis Carroll, read by Hayley in the Schematic Group. A section from *Charlie and the Chocolate Factory* by Roald Dahl (1967), was judged to be an average text for this age range. Easy texts included *The Ha Ha Bonk Book* (Ahlberg and Ahlberg, 1982) and *The Wriggly Worm* from the *Tiddlywinks Read Together* series. In a few cases the section read aloud was considered more complex than the typical category for the whole text. In such cases these excerpts were placed in two intermediate categories: 'average–demanding' and 'average–easy' as Table 5.1 shows.

Table 5.1: Complexity of text of self selected books

Category	Group	
	Integrated	Schematic
(a) Demanding	12	1
(b) Average–demanding	1	0
(c) Average	12	8
(d) Average–easy	2	3
(e) Easy	9	23
Total	36	35

Table 5.1 reveals the variety in complexity of texts chosen by children in both groups. Two categories account for the biggest differences between the Integrated and Schematic Groups. These were the 'easy' and 'demanding' categories; there was a smaller difference in the 'average' category.

The most popular category was 'easy', chosen by 32 of the 71 children whilst only 13 brought texts of a demanding nature. Twenty-three children in the Schematic Groups chose an easy text compared with only nine children in the Integrated Groups. It is, of course, possible that the prospect of reading to one of us may have influenced children in the Schematic Groups to bring a book that they felt safe with. Subsequent discussion with the children, however, elicited the fact that the majority of them, in both groups, had brought the book that they were currently reading in their classroom, although not necessarily the one that they were reading to their teacher. It therefore seems likely that it is the school which influences the choice of book made by these pupils. This suggestion is reinforced by the findings of Nomiku (1991) who demonstrated that teachers are the single most important influence on children's choice of books. Further evidence for the influential power of the school is offered by analysis of titles of chosen books, which shows that out of the 'easy' books chosen by children from the Integrated Groups, two of the nine titles were from structured reading schemes, while out of the 23 'easy' books chosen by children from the Schematic Groups, 19 were taken from structured reading schemes. The indication is that some children may be restricted to a less challenging range of texts by their school environment. Reading scheme books are, after all, designed to make reading easy, yet have been criticised for making reading more difficult (Chall, 1983; Bettelheim and Zelan, 1991). Southgate, Arnold and Johnson (1981) also raised the possibility of books read by children to their teachers being too easy and possibly hindering children's progress. Evaluative work by Chall, Jacobs and Baldwin (1990) places particular emphasis on the need to provide challenging books to ensure reading development.

Twelve children in the Integrated Groups chose 'demanding' books to read, compared with only one in the Schematic Groups. None of these books was from a structured reading scheme. This wider choice from books made available in school suggests that these children have more confidence in themselves as readers and are willing to take more risks in their choice of reading materials.

Choice is an important factor in reading, as it contributes to children's motivation. If, for example, a child is interested in astronomy and already knows many of its concepts, a demanding book can be tackled with enthusiasm and likely success. Early student participation in the selection of reading material is considered an important component of the reading process (Meek, 1982). Our analysis suggests this is also true for children beyond the age of seven who are still working towards reading at an independent level.

There are, of course, problems associated with demanding texts. These children were chosen for the study because they were perceived by their teachers as having reading difficulties, yet some of them chose books considered to be 'demanding' for average readers of their age. Little is to be gained from choosing over-demanding books, if the ability to read and understand the books is lacking. Progress is not made without support from both text and teacher. We obtain a further perspective on the issue of reading with understanding in our assessments of accuracy and fluency.

Accuracy and Fluency

While a standardised test can be used to assess accuracy and comprehension, it is not really profitable to measure reading fluency in terms of time taken to read a passage (Neale Analysis of Reading Ability). Fluency is important to the communication of meaning in reading aloud for a particular audience and is part of the performance aspect of reading, but it is meaningless to measure it in minutes and seconds. Instead we assessed children's accuracy and fluency from their reading of their chosen book to a prospective audience after they had prepared and 'rehearsed', as any performer would be able to do. Assessment of accuracy and fluency of their readings was checked by two judges who listened to the tape recordings. We devised five criteria to categorise the way children read. These were:

- mainly accurate and fluent;

- mainly accurate – where the reading had few errors but was not confident;

- mainly accurate with hesitation – where the flow of the reading was more disturbed, for example, by the reader frequently working out a word through phonic analysis or the use of contextual cues;

- mainly inaccurate and hesitant – where the strategies used to make meaning were not sufficient and help was needed to avoid the reading breaking down;

- hesitant and stumbling – where the inaccuracies were sufficient to break all fluency in the reading.

These criteria are used in Table 5.2 to present findings on our sample of 71 recorded assessments.

Table 5.2: Categories for reading aloud

Category	Group	
	Integrated	Schematic
Mainly accurate and fluent	9	4
Mainly accurate	13	14
Mainly accurate and hesitant	10	5
Mainly inaccurate and hesitant	2	10
Hesitant and stumbling	2	2
Total	36	35

Although Table 5.2 shows that 32 children in the Integrated Groups tend to read more accurately than children in the Schematic Groups (23) the data cannot reveal a great deal about the children's level of reading unless the complexity of the text being read is also taken into account. It is important, therefore, to consider the results of judgements of accuracy and fluency in conjunction with levels of text difficulty.

The twelve demanding texts chosen by the Integrated Groups gave the following breakdown of categories for reading aloud. Four readers were mainly accurate and fluent; three were mainly accurate; three were assessed as mainly accurate with hesitation and two as mainly inaccurate and hesitant. The single child in the Schematic Groups who chose a demanding text was assessed as mainly inaccurate and hesitant in her reading of *The Walrus and the Carpenter.*

The Integrated Groups were, in the main, accurate in their reading of demanding texts, although three of these were hesitant in their reading, needing time to puzzle through context or to use their word analysis skills, and the reading of two more was mainly inaccurate and hesitant. The results do not suggest that children in the Integrated Groups are in danger of choosing texts that are inappropriate for their reading ability.

Table 5.2 shows that the Integrated Groups had more children than the Schematic Groups who were both accurate and fluent (9 compared with 4). The 'mainly accurate' category differs only by one. The main difference, however, lies in the types of text which fit into the reading assessment. The Integrated Groups' 'accurate and fluent' category includes a range of difficulty with four 'demanding' texts; three 'average'; one 'average–easy'; and one 'easy'. None was categorised as 'demanding–average'.

In contrast, the four 'mainly accurate and fluent' readers from Schematic Groups were all of 'easy' texts. The 'mainly accurate' category shows a range for both groups. The Integrated Groups have a wider range than the Schematic Groups, where readings were restricted to categories between 'easy' and 'average' as Table 5.3 shows.

Table 5.3: Texts of 'accurate and fluent' readers

Category	Group	
	Integrated Groups	Schematic Groups
Demanding	2	0
Demanding–average	1	0
Average	7	7
Average–easy	1	1
Easy	2	6

Interestingly, no 'demanding' or 'demanding–average' texts were chosen by the Schematic Groups. Overall, therefore, it is evident that the Integrated Groups were more 'accurate' when reading texts of a generally more demanding nature than were the Schematic Groups. This is also evident when the reading is 'accurate but hesitant', that is, where the children were experiencing slightly more difficulty in decoding the text. This category of 'accurate but hesitant' had also included a range of text difficulty for the Integrated Groups. Four 'accurate but hesitant' readers had chosen 'demanding' texts, two had chosen 'average' and four had chosen books categorised as 'easy'. On the other hand, all 'accurate but hesitant' readers in the Schematic Groups had chosen texts that were categorised as 'easy'.

The Integrated Groups, therefore, are shown to be generally more fluent and accurate in their reading aloud than the Schematic Groups while, at the same time, reading more difficult and demanding texts. In addition, the previous chapter has shown that more children in the Integrated Groups were able to read these texts with appropriate intonation.

50

Summary and Conclusion

Results of our assessment of children's preferred reading texts indicate that children in the Integrated Groups, on the whole, chose more demanding books than their peers in the Schematic Groups and read these books with more accuracy and fluency. School context and previous reading experiences have an important role to play in determining these differences. An integrated approach to the teaching of reading, according to this evidence, appears to produce more confident, accurate and fluent readers.

CHAPTER SIX
Attitudes and Response to Literature

Children's attitudes towards books are adversely affected when their reading is largely confined to one or two reading schemes.

(HMI Report, DES, 1990, p.9)

Introduction

Attitudes are learned and many attitudes to reading are learned in the classroom, particularly in the early stages of reading development. Chambers (1983) suggests that the ways in which children are introduced to books in the classroom are crucial if long lasting and positive connections are to be made between child and book. Attitudes often affect ways in which people behave (Evans, 1965). Attitudes and performance, for example, are closely linked. If attitudes to reading are negative, then early learning and progression may be adversely affected. The Assessment of Performance Unit Survey (1987) suggests that children who are good readers tend to invest effort to extract meaning from what they have read and reach more mature levels of response to their reading. Poor readers are less flexible in their approaches to text; they have ambivalent attitudes to the written text and do not see it as a source of pleasure.

Such attitudes are pervasive and self-perpetuating. Once low status is attributed towards reading it is difficult to change. A child who has a negative attitude towards reading will not become a committed reader. Fewer books will be read and opportunities to extend the range, to read books for relaxation are denied, as are opportunities to progress.

Many poor readers have a negative attitude towards both themselves and reading. Such an effect on self-concept can set in motion a cyclical effect of poor performance, particularly when coupled with a negative attitude towards reading. It has been shown (McKinlay, 1990) that children with reading difficulties have less positive attitudes towards reading than children who are 'normal' readers.

Children's attitudes to reading reflect, not only whether they are able to read, but also whether they choose to do so currently and in the future. Cadman (1983) shows that an interest in reading in early adolescence depends upon habits formed, and voluntary reading done, in the primary school. The survey conducted by Whitehead et al. (1977) suggests that the 14 year olds in his study who had not read a book during the previous month did not regard reading as a source of pleasure or something they would choose to do; this was more prevalent in boys (40 per cent more) than the girls.

Attitudes, therefore, play an important part in readers' development, particularly if they are struggling readers. We were interested in the attitudes and the responses to their books of our two groups of readers and whether there was any difference between the groups.

Attitude Assessment

We assessed attitudes through an attitude test and group activity questions at the initial and final assessments to determine differences between groups and changes over time.

We started the assessment procedure by working with the children as a group to promote informality and confidence. After an initial activity children drew the appropriate faces; 'smiley', 'I don't mind' or 'miserable' (see Chapter 3) in response to four situations:

- watching TV
- drawing
- playing
- reading.

A 'smiley' face represented a positive response, an 'I don't mind' face represented a non-committal response and a 'miserable face' a negative response.

Results show little difference between groups. The Integrated Groups are slightly more positive than the Schematic Groups at the beginning of the study (16 positive and 11 negative as against 14 positive and 20 negative). At the end of the study the situation is similar (for the Integrated Groups, 12 positive and 8 negative; for the Schematic Groups 9 positive and 13 negative). Interestingly both groups substantially move towards a non-committal stance (by the end of the study the non-committed readers in the Integrated Groups had increased from 12 to 19, in the Schematic Groups the increase is from 5 to 17). This is consistent with the results of Wade and Cadman (1986) whose research reveals a similar trend over time towards less commitment to reading.

The attitude test, as Figure 6.1 shows, had 12 statements designed to explore children's attitudes to reading further. Figure 6.1 shows the scores for each of three possible responses. We read each statement to the group and individuals responded on a pre-set answer paper with ticks if they agreed with the statement, straight lines for 'perhaps' and crosses if they disagreed.

Figure 6.1: Attitude Test and Scores

	Agree	Perhaps	Disagree
1. I am a good reader	3	2	1
2. Watching TV is better than reading	1	2	3
3. Books make good presents	3	2	1
4. Time passes quickly when you are reading	3	2	1
5. Anything is better than reading	1	2	3
6. Books are boring	1	2	3
7. A library is a good place to go to	3	2	1
8. The words in books are too difficult	1	2	3
9. Reading is very important	3	2	1
10. I only read if I have to	1	2	3
11. I like reading	3	2	1
12. Reading makes me unhappy	1	2	3

We collated differences for every child in each group and subjected results to one way Analysis of Variance and t-test. However, the tests revealed no significant difference between the two groups. We therefore decided to examine individual statements to determine whether trends in attitude change were discernible even if non-significant. We found two trends from the initial to the final test. Some statements showed a trend towards non-committal, as in the 'smiley faces' test, and others showed a trend towards the positive. There was no movement towards negative responses.

(a) Trends towards non-committal

Statements that moved towards non-committal were:

1. I am a good reader
2. Watching TV is better than reading
6. Books are boring
8. The words in books are too difficult
10. I only read if I have to

Even so, there was no discernible difference between groups, so the information that follows relates to all children in Schematic and Integrated Groups.

I am a good reader

At the end of the study, although the group response was positive, fewer children regarded themselves as good readers. The 47 initial positive responses declined to 39, while negative responses remained on 12. Initially there were 19 non-committed responses, but this rose to 27. Of course, it is possible that modesty or defensiveness influenced responses. Claire, in the Schematic Group, was non-committal in her response, but added:

> everybody says I'm good

Watching TV is better than reading

The main trend over time was towards a less committed stance to both reading and television with the initial nine non-committed responses rising to 24. Those considering TV better declined from 39 to 28 while those considering reading better declined from 30 to 26.

Although our pilot study revealed no problem, the word 'better' might have been ambiguous for some children. Certainly watching TV is *easier* than reading and, as Hughes (1991) suggests, takes up more time. One boy who indicated a non-committal response on the final attitude test remarked to his neighbour:

> I like watching TV but I like reading books better

Books are boring

The trend for this response was strongly away from the negative to non-committal. Initially, 43 thought books boring, but this number declined to 25; the 11 non-committed responses, however, rose to 23. Interestingly six more children recorded positive responses that books were not boring. Some of the non-committed responses actually revealed a thoughtful response:

> it all depends what it is (Darren, Integrated)

The words in books are too difficult

There was a strong move towards non-committed (rising from 29 to 46). The results of interviews (see Chapter 7) suggest that children's focus of difficulty is on 'words', but many of these children have developed strategies over time to deal with them. If, however, lexical difficulty is too great, it leads to a higher number of oral reading errors which may hinder progress (Imai et al., 1992) and, in turn, affect attitudes. Inevitably, as children work their way, either through a scheme or towards more demanding literature, words become more complex. By the end of our study only 11 thought words too difficult, whereas 20 had previously done so; however, the number saying words were not too difficult in their books also declined from 29 to 21.

It may be that the three point scale encouraged some children towards the middle course:

> some are/I'll put I don't know (Laura, Schematic)

I only read if I have to

These responses indicate that, despite the frequency which children say they read at home (see Chapter 7), both groups view reading as less of a priority as they get older. Initially 43 children disagreed with this statement, whilst finally 29 did so. However, the 29 who agreed with the statement initially rose to 33. The non-committed responses rose from 6 to 16.

It appears that many children view reading as something they have to do, or are expected to do by parents and teachers, not as something that they take responsibility for themselves.

(b) Trends towards the positive

The statements that revealed a positive trend over time were as follows:

3. Books make good presents
4. Time passes quickly when you are reading
7. A library is a good place to go to
9. Reading is very important
11. I like reading
12. Reading makes me unhappy

Books make good presents

This statement produced an enthusiastic response with 45 initial positive responses increasing to 55. Typical responses were:

> books are wonderful presents (Angelina, Integrated)

Since most children said books were good presents, it is likely that reading is considered an enjoyable activity; certainly for most children it made the time pass more quickly.

Time passes more quickly when you are reading

The increased positive response (from 36 to 43) shows an increased number of children find reading an absorbing pastime. Eighteen children, however, remained unconvinced:

I wish it did (Ian, Schematic)

A library is a good place to go to

When we talked with children in the interview following the attitude test many of them said how much they liked quiet places to read where they were not disturbed by others. Children's responses to this statement (52 initial positive responses increasing to 71) suggest that libraries are quiet places to go to.

Reading is very important

Initial responses (63) increased to 71 at the final assessment. Only two children in the final session did not agree with this statement. Other children's comments as they filled in their response sheets showed how strongly they felt about this item:

definitely/that's the whole point of why you learn/if you can't read you can't learn/you can get a lot of information from books (Jaspal, Schematic)

I agree with that/otherwise you don't learn anything/when I was on my three day course for the violin I had to read the fire instructions (Marie H, Integrated)

Through schools and the media, messages are given that, in today's society, reading is very important; this message was clear to the children in our research. They were also beginning to understand the wider purposes of reading as well as taking an interest in literature; they saw reading as an aid to learning in that it could impart valuable information.

I like reading and *Reading makes me unhappy*

We present these statements together as, unsurprisingly, they show a similar trend. Initial responses to 'I like reading' increased from 49 to 55, while 14 fewer children said it made them unhappy.

Generally it appears that both groups were beginning to like reading rather more, although 20 children still said reading made them unhappy and 13 said they did not like it. Jonathan, however, gives the majority response to 'Reading makes me unhappy':

of course it doesn't

(c) Summary

Although the results of the attitude tests showed no significant differences statistically, they still reveal interesting trends. Generally, there is a strong move towards positive or less committed attitudes to reading and away from negative views. This general conclusion, however, should not be allowed to divert attention from the minority who still hold negative views. Our research shows the importance of investigating attitudes of individuals, so that the information gained can be used productively in providing for children's needs. As we have shown, some of the information gained was contradictory. There was a move to less certainty as to whether watching TV was better than reading, yet fewer children considered that their books were boring. There was a growing uncertainty as to whether they were good readers, yet more children considered books to be important. More said they liked reading and more considered that books made good presents and that time passed quickly when they read them. More children thought libraries were good places to go to.

The somewhat contradictory responses may be that answering questions in a group encouraged children to comment and consider their responses in relation to group responses. A more refined, 5 point scale might have been preferable for these children; on the other hand it would have been more complex for a sample described as having reading difficulties.

Reader response

At the final assessment we spoke to children about the books they had chosen to bring with them. Individual responses to the books that children were reading gave us an indication of how they were reacting to a particular book and gave us opportunity to assess their depth of response.

Talking about their books was the final element of the assessment and interview session. We were interested in the children's development as responders to text; an important aspect of their development as readers (Protherough, 1983; Fry, 1985; Corcoran and Evans, 1987; Thomson, 1987, 1992). We did not want response to be merely a test of memory or comprehension, but an opportunity to talk freely about a book. Each child came with a friend to make the session informal, relaxed and as much like an ordinary conversation as possible. The emphasis was upon encouraging talk at length in order to infer how children responded as readers.

We tape recorded 61 children's responses for later analysis. Some children in both groups were either unwilling to provide a response or were inaudible on tape. We analysed responses of 30 children in

Integrated Groups and 31 in Schematic Groups using an adaption of the model proposed by Protherough (1983). He categorised responses made by 1,000 children between the ages of 11 and 16. We adapted Protherough's category system to suit the younger children in our study.

Children in Protherough's sample had responded to questions about a specific text; the children in our research brought a range and variety of texts. Therefore, we could not ask specific questions, as in the original research. We decided, therefore, to initiate children's responses by asking: 'Tell me about your book' (which, as Chambers (1985) proposes, suggests a collaboration and a desire on our part to know what they thought about their books) with encouragement during subsequent discussion to relate to 2 of Protherough's 4 modes.

The specific questions he asked related to 4 modes:

- Theme: an awareness of the essential structure of the narrative

- Empathy: the ability to read characters and to enter into their situation

- Motivation: the ability to understand why people in certain situations act as they do

- Prediction: the ability to comprehend likely outcomes beyond the story in terms of the text.

We could not assess our children's understanding of a motive in the book if we did not know the book ourselves; comparisons between groups on this mode, therefore, were not possible. Similarly we could not assess how well children could make predictions from what had gone before. Therefore we decided to concentrate on theme and empathy and our analysis of responses is confined to these two modes.

(a) Theme

We adapted Protherough's 5 levels of analysis for theme into 3 levels more applicable to our younger children.

Our 3 levels of response were:

Level 1. No response about the narrative.

Level 2. A brief response relating to one or more event; 'it's about' the main character or an account of one or more events; comparable with Protherough's Levels 1 and 3 (a particular idea or a vague or unfocused statement which could relate to a number of stories). His Level 2 concerned accuracy which was inappropriate, since our children responded to a wide variety of texts.

Level 3. An extended account describing one or more causal relationships, comparable with Protherough's Level 4 which asks for an accurate or thematic summary.

A distinction is made between Levels 2 and 3 as the ability to logically sequence events is recognised by Stein and Glenn (1979) as a more highly developed skill in the telling and retelling of stories than the mere ordering of events.

Our analysis showed that childern in Integrated Groups generally made more mature responses than those in Schematic Groups.

Level 1 responses

Thirteen children in the Schematic Groups were confined to Level 1 responses compared with only two children from Integrated Groups. Seven of the 13 children in the Schematic Groups were unable to give a resume, although they all brought a text of which, as their reading cards indicated, they had read a substantial amount:

> well you know this cat/I can't think (Navdeep, Schematic)

Navdeep is bilingual with English as his second language. His cultural experiences are not traditionally English yet his reading material in school is based on *Through the Rainbow* reading scheme which features a 1960s middle class family living in suburbia. This is irrelevant for many children in inner city schools but particularly so for Navdeep, making his opportunities for interaction with, and understanding of, the text very difficult.

Another six children in the Schematic Groups, who were unable to give a resume, brought books from a reading scheme which had incomplete extracts from literature rather than whole stories. Possibly this may have affected their ability to retell the narrative content, as they had not engaged in sustained reading of complete stories, a process which may give more opportunity to interact and reflect.

Level 2 responses

Twenty children (10 Integrated, 10 Schematic) gave brief resumes of the text. Five children (3 Integrated, 2 Schematic) responded with one event:

> the boy put a kipper in the teacher's desk (Ian, Integrated)

> it's about different stories/about Goliath and Daley Thompson (Peter G, Schematic)

Others related two or more events:

> it's about Harry/and he has the hiccups and he gets into trouble
> (Matthew, Integrated)

Although Matthew's account recounts more than one event, any causal connection is implicit.

The recounting of events with an explicit causal connection was assessed at Level 3.

Level 3 responses

Eighteen children from the Integrated Groups and eight from the Schematic Groups were able to make Level 3 responses. They were categorised by a detailed retelling of the story; sometimes the whole plot:

> there was a quiet night and the stars were out/and the old dog was thirsty *so he went to get the water can/* and he got his head stuck in the water can and he couldn't pull it out/*so he tiptoed to the window* in the moonlight/and he saw this strange animal and/he woke up a second farmer and said wake up wake up/there's a strange animal attacking our shed/and the second farmer waked up and jumped from his bed and waked the third farmer/he said get up get up there's a strange animal attacking our/shed *so the third farmer got dressed* and put his clothes on the wrong way round/and the first farmer said we can't leave the old dog behind/*because the monster will get him*
> (Jaimini, Integrated)

This story continued at some length! Although English is her second language, Jaimini has successfully recounted four causal connections (italicised) in the extract from her story. This was clearly a memorable text for her, one that she recollected and retold with enjoyment. The ability to recollect is an important step in reader response (Fry, 1985) where the reader is able to fix the story in the memory and, in so doing, feel 'satisfyingly in command of the whole' (p.105).

The results about theme show that more children in the Integrated Groups are able to give more complex retellings of the books they have read, including making causal connections within the text. Realisation of causal connections indicates understanding of the meaning conveyed by print and further suggests that interaction with the text has been fruitful. Obviously a resume of the narrative is reliant partly on memory, but memory is reconstructive rather than reproductive; in this way learning and story become meaningful to the individual and is more successfully retained and retrieved (Ausubel, 1971; Bruner, 1966). The responses indicate that the text has been meaningful to the reader and chosen and read for enjoyment.

(b) Empathy

Protherough had asked, 'Which of the characters do you feel most sympathy with and why?' and had elicited 5 levels of response. We decided not to ask this specific question, but to encourage more general responses. We encouraged children to talk about characters they either liked or disliked, and to say why. Their responses enabled us to use some of Protherough's levels of response with adaptations to others. Our levels were as follows:

Level 1. No response.

Level 2. Mention of a character but with no extended comment, comparable with Level 1 of Protherough's model.

Level 3. A reason for the mention of the character as evidenced from the story, comparable with Protherough's Level 2 (responses in terms of action which reflect on one detail from the story).

Level 4. Makes judgements about actions through reflecting about a characteristic (for example, 'they're bullies') or by making links with personal experience. Although this level does not specifically address empathy towards a character it is broadly comparable to Protherough's Levels 3 and 4, where the reader is able to enter a character's situation or focuses on the feelings aroused in the story.

Our analysis shows that children in the Integrated Groups revealed a greater tendency to give more detailed and complex responses when talking about characters from their texts.

Level 1 responses

Eighteen children (4 Integrated, 14 Schematic) made no comment about a character. Two of the children, one from each group, were unable to talk about character, as they were reading from information books.

Level 2 responses

Twelve children (4 Integrated, 8 Schematic) made a Level 2 response. Some gave a character but could not give a reason even when prompted:

I don't know/she's the main person (Kerry, Integrated)

Level 3 responses

Thirteen children (8 Integrated, 5 Schematic) gave a reason for their choice of character from an incident in the story:

Rapunzel/she looks nice and she says/like/when the prince comes up/she says wouldn't hurt my hair and things like that (Elisha, Integrated)

the iron man/because it shows you pictures where he falls off the cliff and he builds him back up (Michael, Schematic)

Interestingly 6 out of the 13 Level 3 responses show the influence of picture cues in guiding the children's perceptions of character as they refer to 'looking nice' or 'looks cute' or make explicit reference to the illustration.

Level 4 responses

Eighteen children (14 Integrated, 4 Schematic) gave Level 4 responses which included a summing up of characteristics, for example, success or heroic qualities:

I like Romany Rat/he's supposed to be a hero (Emma, Schematic)

professor/he's successful/he's building a mouse trap because all the mice are going into his house (Peter N, Integrated)

Others indicated that they had internalised messages and motives from the text:

Goris/he's the main person/I'd like to be him/he's always on the page/I know him (Gareth B, Integrated)

Gareth's response indicates an understanding of character and motives; this understanding has enabled him to empathise with the character to such an extent that Gareth 'knows' him.

Our analysis of response to character suggests that nearly half of the Integrated Groups (14) are responding at a level which indicates a more personal, reflective consideration of characters in their texts, while only four from the Schematic Groups responded in this way. Other children who made responses in the Schematic Groups either only mentioned a character with no coherent explanation (8) or responded in terms of action (5).

(c) Evaluative response

We used another tool for analysing response, also based upon the work of Protherough. We were interested in children's informal comments about their chosen book. Protherough had noted three stages of evaluation in the 'hundreds of responses made by Hull children to stories they had just heard'. We adapted these three stages to meet the ages of our children and formulated 4 levels of response for evaluative comments:

Level 1. No response.

Level 2. A one-phrase evaluative response, such as an unqualified assertion or a preferred quality; for example, 'good', 'interesting', 'exciting', 'funny'.

Level 3. An evaluative response such as in Level 2 but giving a simple reason, usually in terms of the child's own interests, for example:

it's short and I like it (Adam L, Schematic).

Level 4. A more detailed reason given for the evaluative response, indicating a relationship between the reader and the text where a personal response to the text is the basis for assessment; for example, 'it's good because the man wins and everybody gets their money back'.

Our Levels 2 and 3 are described by Protherough (1983, p.40) as the most elementary stage of evaluation for 11 year old children, although Southgate, Arnold and Johnson (1981) found younger children in their study could make similar evaluative responses. Our Level 4 is directly comparable with Protherough's Level 2.

Our analysis showed that children in Integrated Groups reached higher levels in their evaluative responses than those in Schematic Groups.

Level 1 responses

Two children from Integrated Groups and 11 from Schematic Groups made no evaluative comment about their book even when encouraged to do so.

Level 2 responses

Thirteen children (1 Integrated, 12 Schematic) responded with an unqualified assertion or preferred quality:

Kerry: it's exciting
Adult: oh yes/why's that
Kerry: I don't know

Level 3 responses

Twenty-two children (16 Integrated, 6 Schematic) gave Level 3 responses, although not all were positive:

it's all right/but it's not an imagining book (Steven P, Schematic)

it's about this boy who goes on a bus/and he goes all round the city and he can see all kinds of building sites/harbours and airports and countryside and so on/crappy stuff/it's boring (Declan, Schematic)

Books that do not invite the reader into the 'Literacy Club' (Smith, 1988) cannot expect to be positively received. The book that Declan was reading (*All Round The City*, Ginn 360 series) has a forward moving text, but little else. Declan would rather read books about space (see Chapter 7) but is not allowed to make choices in his school, as reading is restricted to reading schemes.

David, on the other hand, enjoyed his reading scheme book:

> well/it's a good book/it's got lots of interesting stories/some of them are true (David P, Schematic)

He had brought his book from the Longman Reading Scheme that takes extracts from literature as well as true life stories of both historical and contemporary characters. These extracts give the reader chance to operate with a wider selection of literature, although they are constrained in length. It is a pity that 'interesting' extracts cannot also be developed into full texts where interest that is generated can be fulfilled. Such 'toe-dipping' into literature must become frustrating if full immersion is never allowed.

Level 4 responses

More children in Integrated Groups (11) gave the more complex responses for this level than those in Schematic Groups (2). Rebecca relates to her own experience:

> I like this book because it's based on school/they're leaving school/they're like children looking for a school (Rebecca B, Integrated)

Donna gave a detailed, although rather confused, retelling of the story and afterwards made an evaluative comment about its theme:

> it's about a girl/and she likes adventures and she goes to Brownies and she one/lots of things/and she likes her little brother one day/she's Snow White for a day at Brownies because Tawny Owl picked her and the Brown Owl came/cos she had a cold/and she said/Snow White doesn't have a thin face and blond hair/she has a chubby face and black hair/she'd built her hopes up/and she went and told her Mum and Dad and her brother/and she said/my brother was pleased/he had a proper princess for a week/then when she went the next week she said sorry/you're not the part now/and she picked her best Brownie/I didn't think it was very fair on the little girl/to build her hopes up and then let her down like that/cos you don't do that kind of thing (Donna, Schematic)

Donna was able to empathise with the character in the book and generalise from the incident to make an evaluative comment about the morality of the particular situation. She reflected on experience showing what Protherough terms an interaction between the reader and the text, a sense of the book not going 'right' because of its unfairness. This relationship between reader and text is a more mature response level: an awareness that a personal response is a basis for assessment. Donna has a book that enables her to do this. It is a book she has brought from home as her school only used reading schemes.

Other children told us about the emotional effect their book had upon them. Yasser, for example, told us how his book frightened him:

> it's a frightening book/it's about these evil pirates...I feel frightened when I'm reading it (Yasser, Integrated)

Responses indicate that more children in Integrated Groups evaluated their texts more reflectively than their counterparts in Schematic Groups. Longer, comprehensive texts of children's own choice are likely to give opportunities to evaluate more effectively. Additionally, the integrated school contexts showed that discussion of books was an integral and important component of their language policy and practice.

(d) Summary

Our analyses of children's responses are necessarily subjective in part. There are no absolute categories for assessment of developing readers in terms of responses to text. However, there are discernible differences between the two groups of children.

The Integrated Groups, as a whole, are able to talk in more detail and more reflectively about the books they read. More Integrated than Schematic Group members:

- relate the narrative with underlying causal connections;
- are reflective about the characters in the text;
- evaluate the text at a personal level, indicating an awareness of the relationship between the reader and the book.

Higher levels of development may be explained in part by the types and choices of books that children read and the opportunities they have in school to talk about their books in shared discussion. The only school opportunities for sharing a text for children in Schematic Groups was when they were involved in group reading sessions.

Results indicate that many of the Integrated Group and some of the Schematic Group, who were described by their teachers as having difficulties in reading, are capable of responding to literature at least at average levels for their age group.

We concluded, therefore, that all children should have opportunities to read literature that enables them to develop the ability to talk responsively and to reflect. Such literature is personal to the reader and should be chosen from a range and variety of books. Reading schemes on their own offer restricted choice and do not have the range, variety and challenge of books available from book shops and libraries.

Response to literature is also personal and 'special connections' (Fry, 1985) with stories enrich children's reading and enhance development. However, as Fry states:

> Some children never learn to make these special connections with stories and have never learned to expect from their reading something akin to magic. Many of our schools hold a narrow conception of what learning to read entails and of what there is to learn about reading. (p.102)

Summary

This chapter has presented the results of the attitude test and the children's levels of response to their books. The attitude test produced no significant results but we noted interesting trends away from negative views about reading. The analyses of children's responses showed greater diversity between groups. Children in Integrated Groups gave more mature levels of response than their peers in Schematic Groups when talking about their books. We concluded that literature that enables children to respond in depth should be available in classrooms.

CHAPTER SEVEN
What do the Children Say?

I read fact books and story books/I had a big fairy tale book when I was five/I still read it now/I read Roald Dahl/I haven't finished *The Witches*/I've read more but I can't really remember them.

Joseph (age 8)

Introduction

At the interview sessions we properly told children that they were being interviewed so that we could learn from them. The validity of children's views has been established (Deci et al., 1981; Woods, 1990; Wade and Moore, 1992) and elsewhere we have shown that what children have to say provides valuable information for teachers about providing for children's needs (Wade and Moore, 1993a).

Children in both groups were articulate in their responses and gave us valuable insights about reading and the struggle to become readers. In this chapter we go beyond straightforward reporting of numbers; detail of what the children had to say was important and so we include children's comments which illustrate points made.

We questioned children about their reading at home, reading occasions, preferred place and audience for reading, the difficulties they had and what kind of help and books they preferred.

Reading at home

We asked the children whether they read at home. The majority in each group responded positively, although over the study time the number of boys in Schematic Groups who said they read at home decreased (14 to 7). Although these numbers are small and it is therefore impossible to make predictions, it is possible that the 40 per cent of adolescent boys that Whitehead et al. (1977) found read nothing at all from choice may well have commenced their decline in reading at a similar stage in the primary school. If that is so, then school practice which encourages the reader is essential.

Reading occasions

We asked how many times children read each week at home or at school. Some children in each group stated that they did read every day; others read only once or twice a week. A mean score calculation showed that the Integrated Groups read on average 4.4 times per week and the Schematic Groups 3.7 times.

Seven children in the Schematic Groups only read at school. Others more than compensated for this seeming lack of enthusiasm:

> twice a day/once at school and once/at home/if it's Saturday or Sunday I read in the morning and in the afternoon (Clare, Integrated)

> about 5 times at school (USSR) and about 12 at home/I get them (books) from the library (Declan B, Schematic)

Declan did not like reading at school where the reading material did not interest him. His passions are space technology, robots and astronomy but he is not allowed to read books about them. His school had a policy of rigid conformity to one scheme and he was reading on a low level (Ginn Level 6). His teachers complained that they could not get him to read in school; it is hardly surprising:

> I want to become an astronaut/the only story book is my school book/I don't like it/it's crap/I'd like to read space books.

Rigidity of policy may have helped the school identify this boy as a struggling reader:

> 'Special educational needs are not just a reflection of pupils' inherent difficulties; they are often related to factors within schools which can prevent or exacerbate some problems'. The interaction between the pupil and the school, including its curriculum, can also lead to learning difficulties. (*A Curriculum For All*, National Curriculum Council, p.1)

Other activities at home, however, lessen time, and energy, for reading:

> no/I go football training/swimming/football club every day/they all start at 6.30 (Alan L, Schematic)

Preferred place of reading

The bedroom was the most popular place because it removed children from their siblings who were unable to interrupt them:

> on my bunk bed 'cos it's nice and high/and Alex (age 2 years) can't come and rip my book off me (Angelina D, Integrated).

Others enjoyed the quiet:

> in my bedroom where it's quiet/and sometimes I wake up early in the morning/and I've read half a book before I get up (Scott, Integrated)

For some children reading in the bedroom meant getting away from the television:

> in my bedroom/'cos they're all watching the telly/and I need some peace and quiet to read (Stephen, Schematic)

There was a move away from wanting to be in a communal room, especially when there was a television there. In the initial interview ten children said they preferred to read in a room with the television; they had all changed their minds by the end of the study. More unusual places were a car, a wardrobe (with a torch) and the bathroom – all for reasons of quiet and solitude:

> on the loo 'cos I don't like my Mum hearing me read (Jonathan, Schematic)

Although not explicitly stated by all of the children, it does seem that one advantage of being by yourself is that you don't have to read to anybody. In school, however, reading to the teacher is necessary for assessment. The majority of our children disliked reading aloud and the number increased over time.

Children's preferred reading audience

Three quarters of the children (47 out of 78 in the initial interview and 52 in the final interview) preferred reading silently to themselves. Some children (ten each time) didn't mind either way. These figures replicate the results of Southgate, Arnold and Johnson (1981) where three quarters of the children in their sample also preferred reading to themselves.

Our children gave their reasons. For some it was quicker:

> myself/it's quicker (Gareth, Integrated)

Others were concerned about mistakes they might make:

> reading quietly to myself/I think I make less mistakes then/I don't know why though (Joseph, Integrated)

and about the reactions of their listeners:

> to myself/I think it's better/if you make a mistake you make it to yourself and you don't have to read it all again/you can just go on reading and you can work out the mistakes/otherwise you have to read a whole lot again and again (Scott, Integrated)

It is unfortunate that the focus for these children is on mistakes they might make rather than on the content of what they are reading. Smith (1973) and Meek (1989) suggest that reading for meaning is difficult when reading aloud. Comments made by the children suggest that silent reading fosters self correction for meaning; Scott, for example, preferred to go on reading and work out his mistakes without interrupting the flow of his reading.

The reason given for preferring to read to others was the help children could get if they were unsure of a word:

> to other people in case I get stuck (Donna, Schematic)

One boy told us he felt unable to read silently:

> I read aloud to other people because I can't read in my mind (Navdeep, Schematic)

We need to listen to this view, but also to equip children to read for a range of purposes. Restricted emphasis on reading aloud to others, even for reasons of assessing progress, does not give opportunity for children such as Navdeep to develop the skills of a silent reader: for example, faster reading; skimming and scanning; reading ahead of the text to generate meaning from the words on the page. Navdeep may continue to be a child with difficulties in reading despite the extra attention that teachers give him by listening to him read.

Despite their stated preference for reading silently, our children were at the age where they still had to read aloud at school and perhaps at home. We asked them who they preferred to read to when they had to read aloud and who they liked to read to least.

The most popular person in both groups and on both occasions was 'Mum'. A relaxed context was also considered important:

> my grandad 'cos he laughs (Michael, Integrated)

Acknowledgement and praise were factors which encouraged them to read aloud to others. Some preferred more tangible rewards:

> my Mum 'cos if I don't want to do it she says/go on I'll give you some sweets if you do so I pretend I don't want to do it (Brendan, Schematic)

This approach does not necessarily engender a love of reading and possibly makes the work of schools harder, throwing onto them an extra responsibility for fostering positive attitudes to, and interest in, reading.

Major areas of importance for children were caring, understanding and listening:

> my Mum and Dad because they care (Alan, Schematic)

> my mother 'cos she/when I make a mistake she understands me and she helps me get better than anyone else (Emma, Schematic)

> my cousin/she knows what it feels like/she's only 13 or 14 (Matthew, Integrated)

Younger siblings were also popular because they listened and were uncritical:

> my sister and my cousin/they're very small/they enjoy it (Maria, Integrated)

Andrew, from the Integrated Groups, liked reading to his puppy:

> because he doesn't interrupt

Not listening properly was one of the three main areas of dislike referred to by the children; others were shouting or nagging and being unhelpful. Not listening demonstrated a lack of interest:

> my Dad/when I'm reading he's always watching the telly/and he doesn't listen (Laura, Schematic)

Siblings, dads and teachers shouted. Family members shouted at the child:

> not my sister/she nags and shouts at me when I get something wrong/she spoils it (Gregory, Integrated)

whereas teachers shouted at someone else:

> Mrs C 'cos she shouts really loud when I'm reading and tells everyone to sit down (David T, Integrated)

This action would certainly indicate to David that his teacher was more interested in other people's activities than she was in his reading.

More children in the Schematic Groups (21) than the Integrated Groups (16) liked their preferred person because of the help that they were given:

> my Mum because she helps me with the words if I can't quite get them out of my mouth (Ian, Schematic)

Seven children in the Schematic Groups preferred others to sound out words for them.

Children in the Integrated Groups wanted to do the working out themselves:

> my Mum because she helps me out with the words/and she splits it up and she tells me to say the word and I work it out (Gregory)

> my Dad because he never tells me what the thing is/we have to sort it out ourselves (Gaith)

Other children are trying to be independent readers but are frustrated and, as Braun (1985) suggests, confused by the inappropriate help given to them by their listeners:

> my grandad and sister/they get me all muddled up b-a-c/she gets mad at me and she's impatient/he says break it up break it up/you must break it up before you read (Rachel, Integrated)

Schools need to be aware if children are being restricted to one strategy. Children need support when reading, but need to learn a range of appropriate strategies (DES and WO, 1990) which enable them to read to themselves and independently.

Eleven children disliked reading to their teachers. There was an increase from two to nine children in the Integrated Groups at the second interview. Perhaps their move to independent strategies makes them dislike the dependence of having to read to a teacher. One boy in the Schematic Groups who disliked reading to his teacher explained why:

> if I read to the teacher/if I get a word wrong I have to turn the page down and I have to start the book again (Michael C)

Such practice, which concentrates on single words which are incorrect, does not help Michael to appreciate the continuity of the story or to be able to predict (except those bits he has already read). It might also explain why his attitude to reading is negative. Reading aloud is not productive if it is seen as a test. The reactions of these children endorse Findlay's (1986) assertion that the reading activity must be seen to serve a useful purpose, particularly for failing readers.

Children also disliked being told they were wrong and preferred being given the opportunity to sort it out for themselves:

> my relations/if I read they say/you've read that wrong/whereas my Mum will wait until the end of the page or sentence/and then say have a look at this (Matthew, Integrated)

The ability to self correct is one of the first signs of a competent reader

(Smith, 1973) and is seen to be an important and appropriate skill. Children were becoming aware that they wanted to self correct and could do so by using the context and their understanding of the meaning of the passage.

Difficulties and what to do about them

As the children had been selected for this study because their schools considered they had difficulties in reading, we wondered what it was about reading that made it so difficult for these children. Unsurprisingly the answer to this very broad question was 'words'.

> the only thing I find difficult about reading is the words (Leanne, Integrated)

Different types of words gave problems. Little words only caused problems for one child in the final interview:

> I can read the little words but sometimes I can't/when you've read all the big words and you can't read the little words it seems stupid/I feel stupid (Donna, Schematic)

The majority of children who found words difficult in both groups specified 'hard' words, although few could state what they meant by hard words. As in the study by Southgate, Arnold and Johnson (1981), they found it easier to give a word as an example:

> the words are a bit hard/like *adventure* they're hard to sound out (Peter N, Integrated)

Some explained their strategy for coping:

> the long words/I bought a dinosaur book on Saturday/and some of the words are so long I have to split them up/and if I can't get them I have to ask my Mum/and sometimes even she doesn't know (Scott, Integrated)

Some children do not have the strategies to cope:

> I think it's the way I pronounce the words/I can put the letters together but they don't come out right (Peter B, Integrated)

Over-reliance on one strategy can lead to difficulty. Peter's attempt to sound out the words is not working. A strong focus on the teaching of letter sounds and using them to 'build up' words may be an appropriate strategy for short, phonically regular words but still causes problems (Bradley, 1990); 'ker-arh-teh' does not 'say' cat. Putting the letters together simply does not work for long and possibly complex words and is a strategy that gets in the way of reading. Most children are good learners and will generalise learning from specific instances. If they are taught only one strategy they will generalise to all circumstances. A working knowledge of a variety of strategies from the very beginning will allow more children to integrate them and solve the complex problem of reading with greater satisfaction. Children need guidance about the number of strategies they can use to solve their reading problems: re-reading a text to give meaning; reading ahead to get a cue; looking at final or initial letters to encourage the correct word; identification of syllables to help with a word unusual to their vocabulary – all within the context of the meaning of the passage. They need to cross-check using a number of strategies. This is what good readers naturally do to get themselves out of trouble; others have to be systematically taught.

A school policy which gives guidelines to teachers how to teach strategies systematically would save the feelings of stupidity, embarrassment and frustration that some of these children experience, particularly when progress is marked by overt comparison with others:

> if I get some long words wrong/I can't say them out properly/I get embarrassed/the person I sit next to is way past me (Kerry, Schematic)

> hard words/I had a book called the *Karate Kid*/and I felt like throwing it in the bin (Martin H, Integrated)

Some children had worked out methods of helping themselves. They also told us about the kind of help they preferred listeners to give them.

Preferred help

When we spoke with children at the final interview we found that fewer asked for, or wanted to be told, the word. This was particularly so in the Integrated Groups. No child said that they used sounding out the letters as a strategy although a minority asked for that kind of help. It may be that *hearing* others sound out the letters enables easier synthesis of sounds into words. Certainly the children stated that it was not useful when they had to do it themselves:

> my Mum tells me to sound it out/but every time I sound out the word I don't get it right/I'd just leave the word out (Hayley W, Schematic)

As Huxford, Terrell and Bradley (1991) maintain, although children can identify the letter sounds, they are unable to connect them to make words. Fewer children want the adult to read on for them so they can guess the word; they prefer to do it themselves. Taking responsibility for one's own learning is an important step forward.

More children said that they preferred help with the syllabification of words:

> you get your hand and you go like that and it says/rob/then it says/in/robin (Scott W, Integrated)

Some children referred to using more than one strategy:

> I look at the word/and if I can't work it out I read the next two lines/and then that helps me/and if that doesn't help me I look at the pictures and if that doesn't work I go to Mum or Dad (Laura L, Schematic)

Reading on was favoured by some children (10):

> go past it/then usually find out what it is (Joseph H, Integrated)

> if I read on sometimes that helps me/then if I read the next word/I sometimes think that doesn't make sense/but another one will/and that's how I know the word (Claire, Schematic)

Reading on is only productive if the sense can be gained from the rest of the text. In reading aloud the embarrassment of not knowing a word can lead children to devise strategies for negotiating failure:

> I just miss out the word/if I'm reading to Miss J/I do that/I just go quiet or say something else/you won't tell her will you (Gregory, Integrated)

This strategy can only be temporary negotiation to avoid failure, when teachers are not listening sufficiently carefully to notice. Discussion with the teacher, if the social relationship between teacher and child is positive and accepting (Campbell, 1986), enables the child to learn and, at the same time, protects self-esteem as a reader. The difference between merely hearing reading and listening to and guiding reading clearly influences differences in children's progress.

Children's preferred reading text

At the final interview we found that children in the Integrated Groups had moved towards reading a much wider range of texts than children in the Schematic Groups. Twenty-eight Integrated Group children compared with 13 Schematic Group children mentioned a wide variety of books:

> *The Lion the Witch and the Wardrobe* series/adventure/story

books/comics/funny books/poems (Tara, Integrated);

whereas typical Schematic Group responses were restricted to an author (Roald Dahl), a reading scheme (Ginn book) or a genre (annuals). Two children in each group said they preferred information books:

> I like books that tell me things/I've learned a lot about dinosaurs/spiders and things (Lawrence S, Integrated)

and four children in the Schematic Groups said they didn't like anything.

Children need encouragement in school to extend their reading towards encounters with different kinds of imaginative and factual writing. Tindall (1986) asserts that children who read only reading schemes are essentially unaware that there are other types of books for them to read. If variety in school is not made available for children, opportunities for making choices are constrained and opportunities for investigating different texts are restricted.

Nineteen children (15 Integrated, 4 Schematic) gave reasons for their preferences:

> some are adventurous/some make you laugh which I like/some are interesting (Teri-Ann W, Integrated)

Talking about books, as we have said, was part of the integrated schools' policies. Discussion encourages children to become responsive and active readers and able to make reflective choices about the books they choose to read.

There was no consensus as to whether hard or easy books were better:

> interesting books and books that have got a good adventure and they are all/I find if you have an easy book you go through it in a day/and if you have a larger book/it takes a long time and you've got time to think about it I love adventure books (Rebecca B, Integrated)

Others preferred shorter texts:

> I can read them in one go (Diane W, Schematic)

> because they're quicker (Clare B, Schematic)

Everyone enjoys a book that can be read in one go. It is easy to understand why children who have been classified as struggling readers prefer to get through texts quickly, particularly if that is a sign of progress. There is a need, however, for them to be introduced to texts which begin to make demands on them in terms of length and plot but which will also sustain their interest. Access to a wide range of literature gives them this opportunity. Support from, and discussion with, the teacher or another adult sustains enjoyment and understanding. Lack of variety, choice and suitability were direct factors for seven children in the study disliking their books.

Seven children from the Schematic Groups disliked the books they read at school:

> school books/because she doesn't buy new books/and you keep reading them all again (Scott K)

> I don't like the Ginn stories because they're boring when you read them/it's funny/some of these stories have got nonsense (Amber A)

Eleven children said they disliked 'boring' books; six said they disliked babyish or simple books:

> I'm fed up with children's things/they've just got pictures and a little bit of writing/I'd like more words to read (Nigel N, Schematic)

> baby books/they're too easy (Rachel B, Integrated)

Many children dislike being patronised in their learning (Southgate, Arnold and Johnson, 1981; Wade and Moore, 1992) and books which are perceived as easy and babyish give children negative messages about themselves as readers. Particularly if children are diagnosed as having difficulty, needs and interests should be matched with suitable texts if children are not to be turned off reading.

Summary

Most of our children regularly read at home despite access to television, videos and computers. They preferred to read in quiet, solitary situations and to read to themselves rather than to other people. If they did have to read to others, they preferred people who listened and concentrated on what they were reading and who were sympathetic to their needs.

School reading scheme books were not popular as texts; neither were books that were perceived as too easy or babyish.

Children in Integrated Groups showed more independent strategies in reading, using their own variety of skills. They also read a wider variety of books and gave a wider range of reasons for their preferences

We can learn from what these children have to tell us. They need opportunities for quiet times when they are able to read uninterrupted. Many schools operate a policy such as USSR (Uninterrupted Sustained Silent Reading). They also need access to a variety of texts and to have choice in what they are reading. Even in schools where a reading scheme is the main resource, it is essential that children have opportunity also to

78

read outside the scheme and to make choices to match texts with their interests. They need teachers who are aware of the range of literature available in order to extend their choice. It is also essential that children have opportunities to talk about their own chosen books, either to peers or teachers, and to have specific guidance and support when they are reading. Less reading aloud for assessment would also be appreciated by our children. Sharing books and activities facilitates reading practice and the opportunity to extend reading strategies.

CHAPTER EIGHT
Strategies and Comments

this is good this is/my mate Kenny wants to come/can he come an' all/he
wants to do this/it's good stuff

Andrew (age 8)

Introduction

This chapter concentrates on a description of classroom strategies that can
be used to support reading development. We have seen, in the earlier part
of this book, that the traditional way of catering for the needs of
struggling readers is to structure teaching into a scheme of small steps and
easy, graded texts. However, we have also examined the argument that
children require texts that are both challenging and supportive, if they are
to progress and sustain the motivation and interest that makes them
effective, responsive readers. The results we have discussed in previous
chapters corroborate this argument.

As well as support and challenge, another essential of provision for
reading development is responsibility. Provision needs to be structured so
that children take control of the strategies that make them independent
readers. The strategies that follow are whole class activities that we used
to give children some responsibility for their own learning. They can be
used to provide entitlement to a full and varied curriculum in language
and literature and allow for differentiation by outcome. They are
supportive strategies, structured in that they require the supervision and
support of the teacher to enable the child to proceed through what
Vygotsky (1978) described as the 'zone of proximal development': in
other words, for the reader to achieve independently tomorrow what is
done with help and support today. Furthermore the learning situation has
to be positive and enjoyable to allow the child's self-confidence and self-
esteem as a reader to develop and flourish.

Different children will require different amounts of teacher and peer
support, but the strategies and approaches we describe have worked in

group reading and with whole classes of mixed ability.

We now describe the strategies and approaches used in our research over a 15 month period with children designated our Integrated Groups who were in six schools. Although we used the activities with groups of so-called readers with difficulties, they can easily be used with a whole class.

Our aims for all our group sessions were:

- to use peer support as encouragement;
- to encourage individuals to take responsibility for their own learning;
- to tackle reading as a problem solving process;
- to encourage sharing of reading and learning strategies;
- to promote discussion of the text read and of the strategies the children were learning;
- to create opportunities for writing;
- to provide opportunities for consolidating what had been learned;
- to create enjoyment to build and sustain confidence.

As we explained in Chapter 3, we used our seven sessions with the Integrated Groups to provide a check that they received holistic language activities consistent with the integrated policies of their schools.

Our intervention was facilitating and enabling, providing what Bruner (1986) termed the scaffold of learning. We now describe the seven activities that we used with Integrated Groups together with further suggestions for practical extension in classrooms.

Making a Picture Book

This is a strategy that is frequently used by class teachers, but not always one that is often extended purposefully to inexperienced readers in the class. We asked the children to write and illustrate a picture book for younger children to read. Structure was given to this strategy by providing a book for the group to read which had a particular format. In this instance we used the picture book *The Trouble With Mum* (Babette Cole, 1983). The book opens with a statement of what the trouble with Mum is and then gives instances through narrative. Children read the book as a group (one school with ten children in the group were also given *The Trouble With Dad* by the same author) so that they could all follow the text. If one child hesitated over a word, this was either supplied by another child or worked out, using a combination of strategies, by the rest of the group.

The simple and supportive structure of the book promoted success and satisfaction.

During the reading we encouraged children to comment on the text, the illustrations and the sequence of the narrative. Some related the story to their own experience:

the trouble with my Dad is he farts (Andrew)

the trouble with my Mum is she nags (Clare)

with added comments as to why the behaviour was troublesome. In this way children began naturally to explore the language structure of the book.

We then asked children to plan and write their own books, *The Trouble With...*, suitable for younger readers. We gave them the choice to work individually, in pairs or in groups. The majority chose to work in pairs.

Discussion initially centred on choice of character; this was usually a family member including, in one case, the family pet. This talk allowed children to draw upon their own experiences in order to structure their narratives. Many of these experiences were shared with their partners orally, even if they were not included in the book. Once the character had been chosen, they talked about the structure of the plot:

what's going to happen (Matthew)

and used this verbal rehearsal as a first draft of their book. Others made notes to enable them to remember the plot and the sequence. There was the realisation that the text would have to be simple:

it's for the little kids (Clare)

and that the illustrations should match the text:

you'll have to have him sitting down (Peter)

Division of labour had to be decided. In some pairs one member wrote the first draft of the text and the other worked out the illustrations. Others took it in turns to write. They read each other's work to check and to ensure continuity:

what have you said/let me read it first (Jaimini)

and made comments about others' efforts:

that's good/I like that (Scott)

Others grew impatient at the time their partners were taking:

can I have a go (Atiq)

We supplied sheets of A4 paper. As well as the reading, writing and discussion of the text we drew their attention to the practicalities that had to be solved as to the numbering of the pages when children worked simultaneously. Some solved the problem by making a mini-book, numbering the pages and roughly drafting the contents. Others folded their sheets, made them into a book and put the page number next to notes that they had made. These decisions were made as a result of collaborative discussion with peers and, at times, with us.

The majority of books were still at first draft stage at the end of this first session. However, children wanted to finish them and did so either in their own or in class time. At the following session many children reported that they had taken their finished books home to read to their families. Clearly this sharing of their work had given much satisfaction as well as further reading practice. Andrew had taken home his book *The Trouble With Dad*:

> he wasn't very impressed miss

Andrew was referring to content not construction, since his story concerned his father's flatulence. Andrew, however, thoroughly enjoyed the activity, as did the others:

> I like the story we started (Clare)

Commentary

Shared enjoyment in groups of *The Trouble With Mum* supported children's understanding of the chosen text. We encouraged the sharing of reading cues (context and phonic analysis) to make meaning of the text. The children also corrected their reading. Interestingly they corrected the errors of others before they began to self correct. It may be that they were more relaxed when watching other children read and had the opportunity to focus on the text rather than their own performance.

Talk enabled children to share experiences related to the story and to use these experiences as a basis for their written narratives. These, in turn, encouraged the children to organise their writing to follow logical and causal sequences. Discussion during and after the reading enabled children to explore characterisation, plot and structure and, furthermore, to make this awareness explicit. They also demonstrated knowledge of how books work and how they differ in terms of format and language for different audiences. If all children have this awareness, no wonder they feel patronised or see themselves as failing readers when they are offered texts which have been pared down in terms of vocabulary and language complexity to make reading easy for them.

These children appreciated humour in the texts and the majority ensured that there was appropriate humour in their own stories. They also commented positively, critically and evaluatively about the stories their peers had written and they offered advice:

> I don't think your Mum would do that/she's not that daft/I'd change it (Maria)

Many other books can be used as a starting point and as models for book writing. Their structures act as guides for children's writing. Examples of such books are:

- *Come Away from the Water, Shirley* (John Burningham, 1977) which has a straightforward narrative on one side of a double page spread and a picture narrative on the other which is quite different. Another title by the same author which follows the same format is *Time to Get Out of the Bath, Shirley.*

- *On the Way Home* (Jill Murphy,1982) where each double page spread provides an ingenious excuse for Clare's bad knee, each more outrageous than the previous. Each excuse starts with the same language structure, providing repetition for confidence and fluency and a model for children's own writing.

- Books which give a narrative sequence without a text provide an excellent structure for children's writing: *The Snowman* (Raymond Briggs, 1980), *The Gift* (John Prater, 1987) and *I Can't Sleep (Philippe Dupasquier, 1990).*

Using existing books as models enables children, who schools describe as strugglers, to engage productively in creative activities. The strategy also integrates reading with speaking and listening, and with writing. Writing books for younger children necessitates reading a large number of different books at that level to ensure that ideas and language level are appropriate. The use of picture books enables inexperienced readers to read supportive texts which are non-patronising and often complex in their ideas. Practice of reading becomes an enjoyable pastime rather than a chore, yet extends both vocabulary and skills. Discussion and writing of books extend children's knowledge of layout, authors, title page, dedication and even the ISBN number. Children are keen observers and, in a relaxed context, avid questioners and learners:

> what's that for miss (Andrew)

> why do they do that (Peter)

Cartoon Sequence

We began this session by reading a short story aloud. In this case it was *Seventeen Oranges* (Bill Naughton, 1968), a story set in the 1950s, which involved the central characters stealing from cargo ships. However, any short story which has a strong narrative sequence is appropriate for this activity which is equally appropriate for whole classes.

The children were asked to recall individually any one event that they remembered from the story which was different from those offered by the other members of their group. We scribed their responses on separate pieces of paper. The papers were then placed on the desk or floor where all the members of the group could see them. The group task was to read the written events and to place them in correct sequence. Once this had been completed satisfactorily, cartoon sequences were drawn to correspond with the events.

Both during and after the story reading, vocabulary (for example, 'depot' and 'evidence') and the slang used in the story (for example, 'on the fiddle', 'knocked one off') generated discussion. Examples of the slang that children used in school and at home provided further opportunities for work on Standard English.

The sequencing of events that children recalled was not always straightforward. There were often questions and challenges:

Shaun: did the cat jump out of the box first
Matthew: you shouldn't have done that one first
Joseph: no/you need the cat story before the eating of the oranges
Lawrence: it comes in between
Scott: the stealing of the bananas comes first

Some of the dictated, written events were ambiguous. For example, 'He was with the horse and cart' could have been placed at one of two points in the story. This promoted lively discussion in one group with an agreed resolution:

well I meant it to go there (Peter N)

As discussion about sequencing continued, there was the realisation that some important events had been missed out. The children insisted that these were included (they also insisted that we drew some of the additional illustrations).

As children drew their cartoons they discussed events and details of the story. There was, for example, attention to the sub-plot within the main story (the stealing of a cheese with the aid of a cat and a box):

he's hiding the box/oh yes/then the cat came out/the cat escaped and the man threw the box out (Anjam)

Details were added to the story:

this is where his friend lives (Gregory)

this boat's from Germany (Kwabena)

he's never going to fiddle again (Ian)

Explanations referring back to details in the story were given about their drawings to us:

look miss/I've given him the dirty look/this time I've got to do him smiling because he's got the cheese (Steven)

look miss/he's crying/he ate so many oranges that he's turned orange (Lisa)

I'll do the pockets with the pockets bunching up/he's got lots of oranges in his pocket (Rebecca)

Children were interested in each others' illustrations and their accuracy:

Yasser: you've done one/two/three...twenty-one oranges
Anjam: no/there's seventeen here
Yasser: there aren't/it said seventeen
Anjam: mind your own business

They were not content merely to draw:

I want to do some writing (Jaimini)

Andrew: we have to do some writing because it's a cartoon
Clare: yes/we can do bubbles when they're speaking

Children included speech bubbles, explanatory notes under illustrations and, in one school, a notice on the head teacher's door: DO NOT DISTURB

Commentary

Listening to the story and the subsequent activity enabled children to participate fully in discussion and to fully understand an intricate sequence of events. Their reading of handwritten notes encouraged re-reading, checking and verification of what had been read in order to ensure that the sequence was correct. Re-reading and constant checking is a strategy that enables readers to progress in understanding and decoding of text.

Opportunities were given to:

● recollect events

86

- sequence written events
- question events to verify accuracy and sequencing
- establish cause and effect
- discuss the use of language, i.e. slang
- make reasoned predictions, for example, 'he won't fiddle again'
- recognise and deal with ambiguity.

The cartoon activity ably demonstrated the children's knowledge and understanding of the cartoon genre. For example, they used writing as an added communication tool in the depiction of the narrative to facilitate clearer understanding. Writing was used for labelling, for explanation and

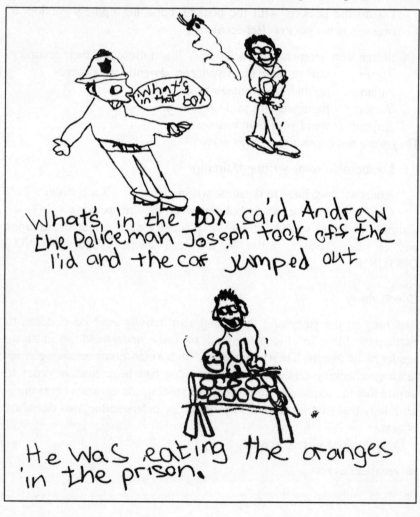

for the depiction of direct speech through the use of speech bubbles. A clear distinction was observed between the writing of direct and reported speech. In one cartoon both devices were used.

There are other ways in which cartoon activity can be used.

- Individual or group cartoon. If children are working on a group cartoon, discussion about the activity includes not only sequencing of events but also continuity factors such as what the characters look like. The portrayal of characters has to be consistent throughout each picture, even when different children are drawing them.

- Individual cartoon sequences of a well known story with the teacher stating the number of pictures to be drawn. Cartoon sequences can then be shared with the other children to compare the choice of incidents and to discuss why those particular incidents were chosen.

- In groups children could decide which are the important events in the story (the number of events will be designated by the number of the group). After discussion each child would be allocated one event to draw. The group's drawings make the cartoon strip. The cartoon strip can be shown to other groups and the choice and sequence of events can be defended.

- Children can write their own commentary of their cartoon sequence and read it to the class. A tape and slide show can be made for group use in the classroom.

The important component of such an activity is discussion about the sequence, the causal nature of the narrative and the characters within the narrative. Discussion encourages children to respond to literature in a natural and enjoyable manner and to utilise reading and writing skills in an integrated context.

Tape Recorded Reading

When children read aloud in the classroom it is often to the teacher who is checking on progress and instructing the children. It is, therefore, for most children, for most of the time, primarily an assessment and testing procedure, one that frequently is not enjoyed. Children who are still inexperienced readers are more likely to find it a chore and a trying exercise, particularly as the reading is usually done 'cold' with no opportunity to prepare or rehearse. As any reading aloud is a performance, it seemed right to give the children opportunity to perform with the benefit of rehearsal and practice.

We took a range of books, from picture books to short stories, into the schools. We asked children to choose a book which they would like to read to younger pupils. We then explained that their reading would be put onto a tape and that younger pupils could read the book and listen to the tape at the same time. Some of the children had story tapes at home and were familiar with the idea of listening and reading. They were also told that they would have time to practise their reading. They were very aware of the importance of this:

> we've got to get it right because they'll be reading the words (Gregory)

There were approximately 25 books to choose from. Most children read most of the books before making their choice:

> it must be one I like because I'll read it better (Maria)

Many books were shared and children read extracts to each other and to us both for enjoyment and rehearsal. When the final choice of book had been made, children practised their reading very thoroughly by reading the text several times. The children used a variety of approaches. They read individually, in pairs and in groups. They encouraged each other and offered advice:

> go slower so they can read it (Elisha)

They helped each other with words and came to us to check the word rather than simply ask what it said:

> does it say (Lisa)

There was an insistence from the children that the text was read appropriately and they asked each other for guidance:

> does it sound right (Darren)

It was left to the children to decide when they were ready to read into the tape recorder. Before readings were taped, children from five of the school groups expressed concern that if the children who were listening to the tape were young and could not read very well they might not know when to turn the pages. Consequently signals were devised (taps on the desk or musical instruments) to denote when to turn the page.

During the taping the children were encouraged to introduce themselves and give the title and author of the book:

> hello/my name is Matthew…and I'm going to read *Not Now Bernard* by David McKee

After initial and inevitable giggling, the children settled to read. When a child was reading into the tape recorder, other members of the group sat quietly following the text and tapping appropriately (if rather loudly) when the page was turned and supplying words (in large stage whispers) when the reader appeared to be stuck.

Commentary

This activity gave children opportunity for sustained reading. Every child read at least five books before they made their choice; others read many more:

> I just don't know/there are so many (Andrew)

Far from being unable to concentrate for long periods of time, the groups of children spent at least half a morning or afternoon just reading, and reading with enjoyment. They also showed that they were very capable of making appropriate choices of books for themselves as readers and for younger children as listeners.

Sharing and practising reading aloud was a natural consequence of the task. The children learned new vocabulary in context and therefore gained both skill and understanding. Children also rehearsed for a particular audience. Their practice showed how they considered their audience to be important and they planned their reading accordingly, striving for clarity, expression and choosing an appropriate story intonation. They checked their reading both to ensure understanding and accuracy of the text. Teri-Ann echoed what many of the children said:

> it's important we get the words right

Throughout the activity the children worked collaboratively and supportively and showed an awareness of:

- audience
- the meaning of the text
- the need for accuracy
- one of the purposes for reading out aloud – enjoyment for others.

They treated the reading as a polished performance and read with interest, understanding, confidence and enjoyment.

This activity could be part of an ongoing class topic. The tape recording of reading need not be restricted to narrative; information books and Maths texts could also be read for younger children. Poetry is a medium that should be read aloud; it could be presented individually or in groups.

Similarly, dialogue within narrative could be shared by a group of readers to turn a narrative into a dramatic performance.

Following Instructions: Recipe

Activities, so far, have concentrated upon narrative in reading and writing. The next activity used narrative as an introduction, but the reading for the recipe was non-narrative and non-chronological. This gives experience of working with a different genre frequently encountered in books.

We introduced the activity with a reading from *George's Marvellous Medicine* (Roald Dahl, 1981). The chosen passage was the description of the collection of ingredients for the medicine and the making of it. The title and the author of the book were given before the reading began, although many children had recognised the book's cover. Others had heard of the book and there was some discussion about what stories Roald Dahl had written:

> I've read most of his books except one (Gareth)

> I liked the witches and the BFG (Gaith)

Discussion in one school focused on the author who had recently died:

> he's dead/ain't he miss (Elisha)

Although most of the children had listened to or had read the story of *George's Marvellous Medicine*, they all enjoyed listening to it again. In one school the class teacher had started reading the book to the class and the children were pleased that they were ahead of the others. Children who did not know the story reacted favourably to its telling:

> I don't believe it (Tara)

and unfavourably to the character of George:

> he's wicked to his grandma/even if she is horrible/he shouldn't do that (Jaimini)

After the reading the children talked about recipes:

> it's instructions for cooking (Gregory)

and about the recipes their parents used. Kwabena recited some of the ingredients that his mother used for a cake (later his mother very kindly wrote and posted the recipe to us). Discussion in all groups centred on the importance of reading and following the recipe very carefully:

my Mum had a disaster (Teri-Ann)

We gave a recipe for Peppermint Creams to all the children. One school group with a larger number of children had two tasks. One group of children had the recipe for Peppermint Creams and a second recipe, for Petits Fours, was given to the the other group. There was an initial reluctance to read the recipe themselves:

what'll we do now miss (Donna)

However, we stressed that they were in charge and that they would only receive help if they had tried to work it out but could not. Children worked collaboratively to read the recipes that follow:

Recipe for Peppermint Creams
Block of fondant
Peppermint essence
Green food colouring
Chocolate strands
Paper cases

1. Knead the fondant until soft.
2. Add a few drops of colouring and knead it until it is an even colour.
3. Add a few drops of peppermint essence. Knead this into the mixture.
4. Roll it into a sausage shape.
5. Cut it into segments.
6. Shape the segments into round pieces, like a button.
7. Dip each piece into water and cover with chocolate strands.
8. Put into paper cases when dry.

Recipe for Petits Fours
5 oz icing sugar
Pink food colouring
Cake cubes
Cherries
Sugar strands
Foil
Paper cases

1. Cut the cake into cubes. They must all be the same size.
2. Weigh the icing sugar and put it into a bowl.
3. Add a few drops of water.
4. Add a few drops of colouring.
5. Using a fork hold a cube of cake over the bowl and spoon the icing

over the cake.
6. Let it run off the cake. Put the cake on the foil.
7. Put the cakes into the cases.
8. Decorate with the cherries or the sugar strands.

After the children read each ingredient, they came and asked for it and it was given to them. Some individual words gave difficulty: 'fondant', for example, was mis-read by some groups as 'fondue'; they were told what the word was. (This is a mistake easily made. In the local supermarket one of us overheard a woman asking for a packet of fondue for icing a cake!) The children asked for an explanation of fondant which we gave. This explanation was reinforced when they used the fondant in the recipe. 'Essence' caused some amusement:

Joseph: that's petrol ain't it miss
Andrew: I ain't eating this if it's got petrol in it

and also needed some explanation for those children who had not taken their holidays in France.

The first word in the instructions, 'knead', proved difficult for all of the groups because of the initial letter 'k'. After discussion some children were able to relate it to words that they knew, for example, 'know'. Those who did not were helped. In some cases discussion moved off the recipe to words that began with a 'k' that wasn't sounded. Tara wrote them all down. In this way specific instruction about silent letters was given to individuals who needed it, but in the context of need to understand.

The recipe for Petits Fours caused some confusion where the group mis-read 'cherries' as 'cheese' but queried their interpretation:

David: what'll we do with the cheese/you can't have icing and cheese
Adult: I haven't got cheese
David: it's in the recipe
Adult: are you sure

A careful and mutually supportive re-reading elicited the correct ingredient.

There was discussion when making the sweets:

Angelina: what's a segment
Gregory: it's like a part of an orange

look/it says sausage shape/that's like this/look at my sausage miss (Lawrence)

sausage shape/look at this sausage shape/is this a sausage shape/green sausages/ugh (Scott)

Children took turns in reading and re-reading the text, helping each other where necessary. Each group read the recipe several times to ensure that they were doing everything in the right order. Confidence grew with each reading. For example, Gaith offered to do most of the reading for his group (although he was not allowed to do all of it as the others wanted a go). The initial assessment had shown that his comprehension of written text was poor; he had been unable to answer any of the set questions. During the recipe reading, however, he read the recipe instructions and then explained what had to be done:

> it says here that you've got to knead/that means you've got to mix it together

> you've got to make a sausage shape with the mixture

Concern was expressed about following the instructions accurately:

> what'll happen if we do it wrong/it'll be no good (Steven)

All of the children determined that they would not miss out any stages of the recipe. Consequently they re-read it several times to check, often from the beginning, with increasing confidence and fluency.

Sessions ended with sweets to take home, requests for the recipe and positive comments:

> this is better than George's/isn't it miss (Lawrence)

Commentary

This purposeful activity places full responsibility for reading and interpretation of reading onto children in a non-threatening, collaborative situation. It underlines the necessity of careful reading and re-reading and focuses attention both on the understanding of the content and the necessity for accurate reading of individual words within that content – strategies which are essential for progression in reading. It also gives opportunities to relate new learning to old and to generalise experiences, for example the word 'knead' to words with similar beginnings.

Children constantly interrogated the text to ensure understanding and correct sequencing of instructions. They sought to confirm what they had read rather than depending on the adult; for example, 'does this say?'. Responsibility for their own reading was therefore encouraged.

Although there was little contextual support as in a forward moving narrative, children were able to read for meaning and comprehension (for example, querying 'cheese' for 'cherries') because they were able to link their knowledge and experience of food combinations with the recipe.

The remarks from the children which have been quoted above ably demonstrate that throughout the activity the children collaborated, supported and learned from each other. Equally important, it was a reading activity which they said they enjoyed.

It may be appropriate here to warn that our children were very kind and insisted that they shared their peppermint creams with us; the recipe does not come highly recommended unless the recipient has a *very* sweet tooth!

One additional observation was that even those children who had heard it before enjoyed hearing the passage from *George's Marvellous Medicine*. A good read is worth re-reading and, as we have seen here, promotes fluency, accuracy and understanding.

Reading and following instructions is a purposeful activity which necessitates careful and accurate reading if an end result is required. There are many possibilities for incorporating this kind of meaningful activity into whole class lessons. It is essential, however, that instructions are followed if the activity is to be seen as purposeful and important by the children.

An approach which incorporates the skills, not only of speaking and listening and reading, but also of writing is to encourage class members to write their own series of instructions for other children to follow. Examples are instructions for making cut-out paper dolls, simple origami, following a trail round the classroom or even tying laces. Children enjoy working collaboratively to follow other people's instructions. Following others' instructions also highlights weaknesses in the instructions themselves which may have to be rewritten for clarification. This can be a useful opportunity for further demonstrating the importance of drafting and redrafting.

Letter writing

Before this session the children had all received a letter from us, as promised, which included a copy of the recipe for Peppermint Creams.

This activity also focused on non-narrative although, as with the recipe, narrative (*The Jolly Postman* (Ahlberg and Ahlberg, 1986)) was used as an introduction. The book details the travels of the Jolly Postman in which he meets characters from nursery rhymes and traditional tales. He delivers some kind of written message to every house he visits and this letter/card/circular is contained within envelopes in the book. The different styles of communication give children examples of different genres and provide models for children's own writing. Most were familiar with the book, although some confused it with *Postman Pat*. Some had read part of it before. Scott, for example, joined in with the surprise beginning:

Once upon a bicycle

Our initial idea was to read the book to the children and invite them to read parts of the letters if they wished. In every school, however, adult participation only lasted until the second envelope, when the children took over the reading completely. They read within their group, looking over shoulders and following the text as others read, until they took their turn.

The Jolly Postman is complex in its ideas, themes and format. Much of the vocabulary is challenging. Several words caused confusion: 'finery', for example, was initially read by Rebecca as 'fairy' but this was questioned by Gaith:

it can't be that

Spellings in Goldilock's letter (written in the style of a young child) were enjoyed, particularly 'conjoora' which the children recognised as misspelled. Abbreviations were questioned. Tara thought that 'B. B. Wolf esq.' meant Baby Bear Wolf until the others corrected her:

don't be silly/how can it/what kind of wolf is it (Gaith)

'Esq.' had to be explained, as did HRH. Subsequently HRH was read as Her (His) Royal Highness in full. There was discussion as to why the postman wobbled:

he's sloshed miss (David T)

Every group insisted on reading the whole book, including the whole of the mini-book of Cinderella. Children supported each other throughout their readings. Michael, for example, was reluctant to read aloud, until he recognised something that he was familiar with. He read the birthday card with the Pat-a-cake verse and his peers joined in, giving him support. Lisa was able to read the advertisements on the circular to the Witch:

these are good miss

Children's insistence on reading every page and line of the book was appropriate, since this practice gave them experience of models that would help them in the letter writing activity we had devised.

After children had finished reading the book, they had to decide on the recipients for letters they were going to write. Children in the first school had total choice, but took so long to make a decision that we gave other groups a more restricted choice. For one child in the first school the choice was easy. Joseph decided to write to his brother and started his letter:

'Once upon a bicycle so they say a jolly postman came one day with a letter for Sam ...'

There was discussion among the children as to the appropriateness of their choice:

you don't want to write to her (head teacher)/you see her every day (Joseph)

Suggestions were made at subsequent schools that children might prefer to write to Children's Television either at the BBC or Central TV These were to be letters of praise or complaint:

'Dear funhouse,

I want to make a complaint because you said that men are better drivers. I am sure that men and women drivers are just as good.

Yours faithfully,

tara...'

'Dear Funhouse,

I think the show is brilliant and I would be really grateful if you would let me be a contestant on funhouse. I think the grand prix and the funhouse are the best games. I never miss a show.

yours faithfully,

gaith'

The children were keen to share their first drafts both with peers and adults:

Mrs Moore/can I read this (Rebecca)

what do you think of this/is it too rude (Donna)

Spellings were important for the final draft and children always made an attempt before spellings were given to them. They also read and commented on each other's final drafts:

that's good that is/she'll like that (Atiq, talking to Yasser who wrote to a teacher who had left the school)

In order for the children to concentrate on the content of their letters they were given headed note paper with their particular school's address already inserted.

All letters were individually addressed and posted, including those to the Queen and Michael Jackson! If possible, the group went out of school together to post them. Obviously, permission had to be obtained from the head teacher to take the children out of school. Matthew wrote a letter to his head teacher asking for permission to go out of school; the signature at the end of the letter is the head teacher's message back to Matthew giving assent.

> Dear mr Dent,
>   we have Been writing
> Letters. please may we have your
> permission to Go with mrs moore to
> post our letters. ?
>   matthew

At the beginning of our following sessions three of our Integrated Groups were very excited. They reported success with their letters to the television companies. Two groups had received written replies and another group had been mentioned on television:

> and he said/he wouldn't read any more of our school again/'cos there were so many (Angelina)

The replies emphasise the purposeful nature of this activity, although when writing to large organisations success cannot be guaranteed. Some children reported replies from individuals they had written to and an enjoyable correspondence was maintained for some time between Scott and one of us.

Commentary

The letter writing activity introduced children to different formats of letters, for example, the formal style of the solicitor's letter, the child's letter and the informal holiday postcard. Repeated readings of the book gave children opportunities for sustained, shared and collaborative reading with a constant evaluation of the text. Listening to others reading, while following the text, enabled children to focus on the sense of the passage and realise when a correction was necessary. It also provided opportunities for furthering their learning, for example, of abbreviations. This learning was accomplished in the context of group reading that was relatively stress free and all individual reading was supported by the peer group. Support and collaboration continued into their writing activities, as they wanted their letters to be 'interesting' (Kerry) and 'read on the telly' (Maria).

The letter writing was also purposeful and directed to a specific audience; they had learned about format and style and used this learning successfully. They also had the expectation that their letters would be read and that they might receive replies. It was therefore a worthwhile, satisfying activity for them.

Children all read each others' letters and so extended their reading practice. Their comments and advice showed that they took this role seriously and were able to understand and evaluate each others' work.

Another book which can be used as a springboard for letter writing is *Dear Greenpeace* (Simon James, 1991). Unlike *The Jolly Postman* it does not offer different formats or layout. What it does do is to trace a dialogue in letters between Emily and Greenpeace about the whale in Emily's garden pond. It emphasises the importance of letters and their response in a humorous and sensitive manner and underlines the fact that letters are written to be responded to and are not just exercises.

Other opportunities for purposeful letter writing include letters to the school or local newspaper about issues in the community that concern children. They can also write to their MP if the issue is of serious concern. Letters requesting information for class projects can be written by children in the appropriate style, as can letters making arrangements for class educational visits. Such formal letter writing will require some teacher guidance as well as opportunities to read letters of similar style and content as models for children's own appropriate writing. Not all letter writing is formal. An arrangement of pen-pals between classes in different schools, or even in different countries, is an ideal way for writing and response to be continued over time.

Story completion

This activity returned to narrative as a means of promoting reading strategies. The main reading activity was to be the reading of each others' stories, although a published story was read to children to initiate the activity. We used one of our own retellings, a folk story from Bangladesh, *Fair is Fair* (Wade, Wade and Moore, 1988), and we read it aloud up to a point in the story where a problem had to be solved. Children then had to provide their solution to the problem. The aim was to give them experience of taking decisions, as an author does, based on retrospective knowledge of plot and character together with predictions about what is likely to happen.

The story is about two old women, Tetan and Boka, who agree to share their possessions. Tetan, however, is unfair in her suggestions as to how they should be shared and Boka is foolish enough to agree to the suggestions. The children commented on the way the possessions were shared during the reading of the story. There were four possessions in all:

1. A house: which they shared equally;

2. A blanket: Tetan had the blanket during the night, Boka had it during the day:

> that's not right/it's hot in the daytime (Steven)

> she's not being fair is she miss/that's spiteful (Yasser)

3. A cow: Boka had the front end of the cow that she fed and watered, and Tetan had the back end:

> the back end of the cow/that's the milk end (Angelina)

4. A field: Tetan and Boka tilled the field and planted the seeds. Tetan had everything that grew above the ground. Boka everything that grew below. The crop was maize (explained to the children as corn on the cob).

As the story unfolded the children became incensed at Tetan's behaviour. The readings were interspersed with their comments:

> Tetan's not nice (Tara)

> Boka's foolish (Kwabena)

Angelina was right about the back end of the cow; Tetan kept all the milk:

> I told you so/she's wicked (Angelina)

The children realised that the crop would be to Tetan's benefit before that part of the story unfolded and were already making plans for Boka:

> she'll have to have something like carrots or potatoes (Darren)

We stopped reading the story at the point where a girl was about to offer Boka advice. The children's task was to specify what this advice was. They had the choice of working individually or in pairs or threes. They talked about their ideas with each other and jotted them down:

> 'The next day Boka went out to the field were the crops were growing and took and took them and ate them. Then she dug a pit and covered it with branches and soil. Then when Titan came to eat some crops she fell in the pit. Boka said she would be let free in a week and

all she had Was bread and water. After a week boka told her to go away and never come back.' (Gaith)

'...the cow...they could share the udders ...' (Leanne)

'...swop the seeds for seeds that gow underground. Don't feed the cow fress grass and it won give milk. In the night get the bakit from tetan so she Don't now' (Andrew)

'The next day before Tetan got up to milk the cow Boka milk it instead and when Tetan came to milk the cow Tetan tried onec but no milk came out. So she lucked under were the milk came out and tried again but the cow done a wee on her' (Gareth)

Atiq and Peter retitled their story as they considered 'Greed' to be better than 'Fair is Fair'. All their versions were read with evident enjoyment and were commented on with enthusiasm. Final drafts were pasted into a group book or put on the wall for display for all class members to read. The children enjoyed the alternative endings, but they also wanted to know what they called the 'real' ending to the story. We gave a copy of the book to each group and it was interesting to see with what enthusiasm and success they read the remaining part of the story.

Commentary

This kind of activity encourages children to predict events within a narrative and also sets a problem that has to be resolved within the parameters of the story. Discussion, during and after the reading, showed that children were able to predict the story's outcomes, foresee difficulties and speculate about possibilities. Support during group reading and discussion enabled all children to share and extend their ideas. They made judgements and assessments of characters and of their behaviour. They showed that they were able to empathise with Boka and demonstrated their ability to solve a problem with a variety of suggestions for plot.

Children had opportunities to draft their work after sharing it with other members of the group. They also collaborated to generate ideas and make them work: some children produced a collaborative final piece of work for publication. Finally, they all had opportunity to read and evaluate the work of others and to complete their reading of the original, published story.

Writing the end of a story is an activity the whole class can share. It is important, however, that the story telling is stopped when there is a problem to be solved. This focuses children's attention onto story structure and encourages an effective resolution rather than additional sequencing of events.

There are other ways to engage children in retellings: for example, telling a story from another character's point of view (say, the wolf's point of view in *Red Riding Hood*), or filling in the gaps of the story (what her mother was doing when Red Riding Hood was having her adventure) or writing another episode for the story (Red Riding Hood's conversation with her mother after her adventure). An interesting variation is to tell children the final part of a story and encourage them to think of what went on before, or even to tell the beginning and end and ask children to supply the rest of the narrative.

Board game

This activity involved the strategies of peer support, collaboration. and sequencing of a narrative. The product, a board game, needed planning, drafting and reading in order to devise and play it.

Sessions began with a discussion about board games. All of the children were able to contribute to this discussion by sharing the types of games they played. These ranged from *Snakes and Ladders* to *Monopoly* and *Dungeons and Dragons*. They talked about the rules that were needed, the board itself and the ways in which the games proceeded. The language of board games was discussed: for example, 'miss a go', '2 paces forward'.

We then read the story *The Pirate Parrot Princess* (Joan Aiken, 1977). Two school groups asked if they could take notes during the story to help them to remember. At the end of the story they had to decide which events they wanted to use as ideas for the board game. They worked in pairs or threes to brainstorm the events and write them down. We made the text of the story available if they wanted to read it. Next, the children had to decide which events in the story were 'good', which they would use to carry the game forward, and which were 'bad', which they would use either to take the game back, as in *Snakes and Ladders*, or to miss a turn. As they were working in pairs, they had to give their partner reasons for their choice:

> if the wind blows them back/that's good/'cos they get changed again (Leanne)

During the discussion they talked about the events in the story:

> I liked the bit where she hit Fairy Grisel on the nose/she was angry/that's why she changed her (David C)

They looked carefully at individual words. Matthew drew attention to the spelling of Jake:

> miss/that could spell Jack/the 'k' would have to go to the end

Donna added events that were not in the story, but which she thought would make it 'more interesting' (we have marked these with asterisks):

find a treasure map go – forward 3*
bump into a tree – go back 1
a monkey drops a coconut on Bill – go back 2*
find a cave – go forward 2*
get blown back to an island – go back 2
find a secret passage – go right to the end*

Darren and Matthew chose their events with care:

- Jake learns to swear – go back 5 paces

- The pirates are shipwrecked – go forward 3 paces (although this was a 'bad' event it carried the story forward)

- The princess hits the Fairy Grisel – go forward 2 paces (again the 'bad' event carried the story forward)

- Jake and Bill stay on the island for 20 years – go back 3 paces

- Jake learns to drink rum – go back 4 paces

- The prince falls in love with Jake's young sister – go forward 1 pace

- Jake and Bill go back to the island – go to end

- Jake and Bill crash into the window – miss a turn

- The Fairy Grisel changes Jake into a princess – go back to start ('because she was a princess at the very beginning miss')

- The princess falls in love with Bill – go to end

- Jake and Bill run a pub – go forward 4 paces

After events had been sorted, the sequence for the board had to be arranged so children numbered their list of events in the correct order.

A grid pattern for the game was made available (to save time and to allow the children to play the game at the end of the session). Most children used it, but others preferred to design their own. Events were written in sequence on the game:

I have to sort the order now (Kwabena)

All children chose to make individual games, even though they had planned together. They wanted their own game to play with their partner and to take home to show their families.

As they worked they commented on each others' work:

oh/that means you're going back to 11 (Maria)

and on their own:

I'm being really mean/when you get to 25 you have to go back to the start (Gaith)

Some of the written events were too long to fit on the squares of the game. Rebecca was one who solved the problem:

I've found a way of making it shorter

She abbreviated her instruction and changed 'The Princess hit the Fairy Grisel with her rattle' to 'Fairy Grisel is hit'.

Next, the children wrote simple rules to accompany their board games. Most children finished the activity before the end of the session. They mounted their games on card and covered them with plastic film. Sessions ended with everyone playing a series of games with dice and counters – and they were fun.

Commentary

Writing down events of the story enabled children to reflect on what had happened and to evaluate events in terms of 'good' or 'bad' for the characters. They also discussed whether events enabled the story to carry forward or whether they were a stumbling block in the narration and talked of which parts they had enjoyed, making their reasons explicit. Those children who used the text of the story to check sequencing of events employed skills of skimming and scanning to find the information they wanted. Our direction was sometimes necessary, but, by re-reading parts of the text and talking about their place in the narrative sequence, they worked out whether the event they were seeking was near to the page they were on.

This activity gave children opportunity to write the language of precise instructions for other children to follow. They also gained experience of writing concisely by abbreviating some of the events to fit the board spaces.

Proof reading was important before the game was mounted and covered as:

it's got to be just right (Maria)

Finally, the children read and followed the instructions for the games devised by others as they played them.

Board games are popular with children and are part of their home experience. Very many different shapes and patterns can be devised and most stories can be used for this activity.

Summary and Conclusions

The activities we chose were designed to enable children to experience a range of literacy activities in an enjoyable and relaxed context. Although narrative provided a supportive, central core for consolidating and extending their reading, the range of texts also included reading (and following) instructions and reading different formats for letter writing. There was also diversity in the range of narrative texts, from picture books to short stories of some complexity.

Five of the activities encouraged the integration of the language modes of Speaking and Listening, Reading and Writing; the recipe and the taped reading involved reading and discussion.

Children's writing included various kinds of narrative as well as instructions and letters for specific purposes.

We consider that the activities had the following benefits:

- The children offered and used a great deal of peer support. This was always positive within all the groups.

- The children began to take responsibility for their own learning in reading and writing, using an adult mainly to check on what they had done with the help of their peers.

- They solved many problems in the reading process; they learned re-reading to ensure accuracy and sequencing; cross-checking their decoding of text by using more than one strategy.

- They shared their learning strategies and made them explicit through group discussion.

- They discussed, reflected about and responded to the variety of texts that they had read or listened to.

- They used opportunities to write purposefully and for an audience.

Observations of the children and notes taken of their comments confirmed that they had found the activities enjoyable (Matthew, for example, said, 'have you come here to help or just to have a good time?') and that their levels of self-esteem were at least positive:

you should have had Stephen as well/he's clever an' all (Maria)

We initially had concern that withdrawing children from their class would produce negative attitudes. Experience indicated otherwise. Requests were made from other class members to join in with the activities. Children regarded themselves as privileged:

we ought to call ourselves the Moore Club/it's good (Elisha)

We emphasise that withdrawal was employed simply to ensure that groups could be compared for our research. For practical learning purposes all of the activities that we have discussed can be used with whole classes where every child can take a full and active role, including, as we have seen, these readers who require extra support.

The children in this study worked well in groups, learning from peers who had experience of different reading strategies. The results of these activities showed that children described as having difficulty with reading can succeed in what they are doing, can make informed and rational decisions about their reading and writing and can consolidate progress in their reading through activities which they find enjoyable.

These children also demonstrated that, although adult help and support is necessary to structure their learning, they are capable of providing help and support for others and of developing self-maintaining reading strategies for themselves.

CHAPTER NINE
Summary and Conclusions

he has a laser gun/and when it fired at a tent with clowns dressed up/lions tigers/they end up messy not very nice is it/I like it when the Gobblewockians come up/I'll see if I can find a bit for you/for example/they don't want Top of the Pops/this one I like most of all/I don't bother to look at all of the pictures/sometimes the pictures are good/this is a funny book/I wonder what would happen if I had aimed his laser gun...I've really enjoyed this/I'd read it again

Maria (age 8)

Introduction

This chapter summarises the results from our West Midlands study and considers their implications for teaching and learning, specifically for supporting inexperienced readers beyond the age of seven. As previous chapters report in detail, over 15 months children in our Integrated Groups made greater progress than our comparable Schematic Groups in both reading and comprehension age. They were assessed as more fluent and accurate in their reading and as using more appropriate intonation. They were beginning to use more independent strategies in their reading, were reading a wider variety of texts and gave a wider variety of reasons for choosing their books. When talking about their texts children in the Integrated Groups spoke in greater detail and with more mature levels of response than did the Schematic Groups.

Progress in Reading

Children in the Integrated Groups demonstrated considerably superior:

- reading age
- accurate and fluent reading
- use of a wider range of reading strategies.

The indication is that factors in an integrated approach lead to such superiority. Children who are inexperienced readers are likely to benefit from skills teaching *within the context of reading and writing*. Our results suggest that the children in the Integrated Groups learned phonic skills, amongst others, and were able to use them appropriately to achieve higher reading age scores which were obtained from a test which assesses skills. Phonics teaching took place in the context of making meaning from texts. Results, therefore, also indicate that inexperienced readers will benefit from reading an extended range of literature, more opportunities to read, purposeful reading and writing and discussion with teachers and peers. They are less likely to benefit from explicit, unrelated skills teaching with limited access to less challenging books, even if they have more teaching in one-to-one and withdrawal groups.

Purposeful activities, which relate to the interactive components of reading, writing and speaking and listening, particularly when they have a designated audience such as the peer group and which necessitate accurate presentation, focus attention onto letters and sounds and their role in word building. As Weaver (1992) implies, this focus encourages readers to think independently. Such encouragement of phonological awareness in purposeful contexts was advantageous for the Integrated Groups.

Our results indicate that, given the chance, children described as having reading difficulties are capable of learning and developing a wide range of skills and using them independently to assist their reading. Building words letter by letter was not a popular approach with the children. Many of them (in both groups) suggested that they found this strategy confusing.

Our interviews with children suggested that those in the Integrated Groups were generally more confident in skill usage; for example, they used their abilities to word build from syllables rather than asking for the word. Our findings question recommendations that children should concentrate on word sounds and phonics (see Wood, 1988) and support assertions that they are taught as one of a range of skills (see Hudson, 1988; Adams, 1990) in meaningful (see Choate and Rakes, 1989) and integrated contexts (Cateldo and Ellis, 1990; Pinsett, 1990). Decoding skills are part of the process of reading for meaning and our research suggests that they are better taught within that process.

Children in the Integrated Groups had access to more varied and more complex reading material written in familiar narrative style with which they could identify. Such materials relate to children's experiences more than the narrow range of subject matter of traditional reading schemes. Appropriate language structures have enabled these children to utilise their extensive knowledge of language in the reading process to solve phonic problems by knowing the patterns and possibilities of language. Literature that has not been written with a focus on phonic or repetitive vocabulary has encouraged children to use a range of reading strategies, including phonics. In literature many words cannot be 'sounded out' (despite some children's attempts), but depend upon either recognising the words or a combination of contextual and grapho-phonemic cues. The results of our research suggest that the more access children have to a wide range of texts and vocabulary, the more likely they are to recognise words, or to use the combination of cues, when they see them in different texts.

Restriction to carefully controlled and limited vocabulary scheme books lessens children's opportunities to meet a range of unfamiliar reading vocabulary. The Schematic Groups' slower rate of progress may be attributed to their not having had the same opportunities as the Integrated Groups to progress, because they have not had the same exposure to a wider vocabulary in a meaningful and motivating context. The word count in reading scheme books is minimal (Chall, 1983; Bettelheim and Zelan, 1991) particularly in so-called 'remedial' schemes, and the language in them is devoid of 'non-context' words that are so important for meaning (Blank, 1985). Similarly, the content that should provide stimulating and motivating reading often takes second place to structure, or is artificial or patronising.

It may be that children in the Schematic Groups, whose reading and comprehension are falling behind achievement levels of children in the Integrated Groups, will be like those secondary school children witnessed by Peters and Smith (1985) who, after six years of phonics, reading schemes and activities, were still failing at reading. Certainly, children in the Integrated Groups chose to read more challenging texts than those in the Schematic Groups. The Integrated Groups had more confidence in themselves as readers, were more competent at making choices and more advanced in their choice of books. Their schools also gave them more time to read: five of the six schools had Uninterrupted Sustained Silent Reading (USSR) sessions, whereas only two schools in the Schematic Groups did so. Opportunities for USSR gave children the same reading entitlement as their peers in mainstream classes in time to read and amount of reading done.

The majority of children in our study preferred reading to themselves rather than to someone else. If teaching focus is on accuracy, concentration remains at the word level rather than on the meaning. Approaches are needed which allow children to read for meaning while, at the same time, not neglecting accuracy. Group reading with peers and discussion about books encourages shared meanings plus a focus on accuracy if the reading is seen as a performance rather than a test. Children have opportunities to rehearse and support each other. These social activities also encourage less reliance on the teacher and enable children to learn useful strategies from each other and to correct the mistakes they make, thus behaving like good readers. Reading aloud is a shared experience in which meaning is central and discussion about text is a natural consequence. Group reading, however, should not be merely used as practice in accuracy for testing by the teacher.

Discussion with teachers also enhances progress. Our research suggests that opportunity for talk is of crucial importance for children who are struggling with reading and who need to progress quickly to ensure that the gap between them and their peers is not increased. It is also crucial in encouraging children to think about their texts and self monitor their thinking (Tonjes, 1988) in a powerful and interactive way (Barrett et al., 1989; Lowndes and Hunter-Carsch, 1989; and Lutrario, 1990). Opportunities to reflect, and to articulate that reflection, very likely enabled children in the Integrated Groups to make more detailed and mature responses about their reading. They showed greater maturity in levels of response than the Schematic Groups and were able to make more evaluative and reflective comments. For example, they gave extended accounts of their chosen stories, gave detailed and reasoned evaluations and were able to talk about characters more reflectively.

Purposeful discussion about narrative and character and the chance to make evaluative responses necessitate access to literature to enable such activities to take place. Our results corroborate what many educationalists and language specialists (Lavender, 1985; Meek, 1988; Wade, 1990) have argued for: the central importance of story in the learning process, particularly for children with difficulty in reading (Simmons, 1987). Our results also support Lutrario (1990), Chambers (1991) and Chall, Jacobs and Baldwin (1990) who argue for a wide range of challenging books which are also good quality literature (Squire, 1990) and which enable children to respond effectively. If children are to develop as effective, voluntary readers, they need books that encourage progress at their own rate rather than limitation within the confines of reading scheme levels.

One of the novel features of our research was analysis of children's use of intonation when reading aloud from a chosen and prepared text. Children in the Integrated Groups were used to sharing their books with other children by purposeful reading aloud. Natural group reading to a 'real' audience seems to have encouraged attention to meaning rather than simply focusing on individual words and has also encouraged the importance of facilitating that meaning for others. It may also be that they chose to read books that they could relate to. Myers (1991) indicates that comprehension is an elaborate process which is dependent on factors inside the text (such as the type and structure of the reading material) and partly dependent on factors outside the text (such as the reader's purpose for reading, the situation in which the reading occurs and the characteristics of the reader). These aspects are not tested by traditional comprehension tests, but the range of measures of comprehension that we have used in this study have been shown to be both effective in discriminating between groups and broadly corroborative.

Implications

Our research was necessarily small scale and exploratory, but its results suggest that, though the majority of 'remedial' reading teaching is skills based (Jansen, 1985), greater progress may be made if children have access to a language curriculum rich in terms of literature, activity and purpose. The Curriculum for English outlines this appropriate breadth and structure and the Curriculum Guidance 2, *A Curriculum For All* (NCC, 1989) importantly stresses the entitlement of all students to a broad and balanced curriculum.

One aspect of such a curriculum is a wide range of literature plus mastery of a variety of reading strategies. Our study has endorsed these factors and shown they enable children to read with fluency, accuracy and understanding and to respond to a text with greater perception. The implication is that all children, therefore, should have access to this wide variety and range of literature that is varied in terms of content, structure and language, together with appropriate teaching. Our research suggests that children benefit from choice in their reading; choice which is meaningful to them as individuals.

Choice is essential to motivation to continue the reading habit beyond classroom walls. The integration of language activities has been shown to be successful in the teaching of reading, but it may also be necessary to highlight reading and to give it visible priority in school in order that progress is seen and maintained. Fostering individuals' reading is crucial and that implies that schools should seek the active co-operation with parents of children beyond the age of seven.

Opportunities for sustained silent reading should be timetabled, but monitoring by the teacher is necessary to ensure that children actually make progress and do not merely flick between the covers. Again the implication is that mere availability of books or strategies for action are not sufficient to cater for the needs of children who have difficulties; emphasis must be placed upon teaching inexperienced readers strategies that they can use independently. Eventually pupils can be taught self-reliance in measuring some of their own progress through reading diaries or reading logs.

The majority of children in our study said they preferred somewhere quiet to read. The implication is that, similarly, in school there should be opportunities for quiet reading when children can become totally absorbed in a book and where reading behaviour is also modelled by the teacher.

Our results indicate that discussion about books and the strategies that readers use is important for children who schools classify as having difficulties in reading. Strategies that encourage discussion, such as those recommended by the National Oracy Project (1990, 1992), should therefore be encouraged and become part of the language curriculum; for example, talking about books with peers or sharing reading in groups. Discussion with the teacher during a reading interview (see Baker, 1984; ILEA, 1988) can be used productively to encourage a greater range of reading strategies. Sustained discussion about texts allows children to use their metacognition and metacomprehension skills (Tonjes, 1988). Inexperienced readers need a metalanguage (paragraph, cross-check, re-read, question mark, etc.) to talk about texts. Talking and reflecting about what children are reading and the meaning it has for them are likely to encourage greater depth of response to, greater interest in and greater commitment to books and reading.

For the teacher, our research implies that diagnostic listening to reading, rather than simply hearing or testing reading, is a necessity, not only to give reading its appropriate purpose and recognition, but in order to check on the reading strategies children are using and discover those they need to learn. We suggest that, if children continue to rely on a narrow range of strategies, the likelihood is that they will remain poor readers. However, children will need teacher help to develop a range of appropriate reading strategies. It is worth exploring ways that encourage such development, before a sense of failure makes progress more difficult to achieve.

Our results show that purposeful reading aloud encourages focus on meaning and use of appropriate intonation. Opportunities should be made in class for children to prepare their reading to encourage a sense of purpose and to eliminate the unseen testing that is usually associated with reading to the teacher. If children are faced with unseen texts to decode publicly, they develop coping strategies rather than independent reading strategies.

Conclusions

From our research a conclusion about method can be safely drawn: the integrated approach to teaching reading enables children that their schools say have reading difficulties to make more progress in a number of measures than similar children who are taught through a schematic approach. However, our results also move towards conclusions about so-called 'struggling readers' themselves. Children with difficulties in reading are not necessarily 'special cases' in need of specialist skills teaching with a focus on accuracy. Children in this study show that they are capable of making gains in skills and accuracy when the focus of teaching is also on meaning and understanding. They may need more attention and support in what they are doing, but this can be supplied in the mainstream classroom with help and support from peers as well as the teacher through discussion and purposeful activities, some of which we have outlined.

Many children described as having difficulties in reading are capable of reading independently and of using a variety of strategies to tackle print if teaching gives them opportunities to do so. They may need more individual guidance in acquiring effective reading strategies and over a longer period of time, unlike competent readers who seem to acquire them easily. They do not need switching from a range of interesting books to simplistic, decontextualised or patronising materials.

Many children described as having difficulties in reading are as able as competent readers to read aloud with appropriate intonation, and therefore understanding, if the activity is made purposeful, if the book is of interest and if they have had opportunity to prepare their reading. Reading aloud does not necessarily have to be to the teacher; it can also be to a sympathetic peer or to a younger reader, if the text is appropriate.

Inexperienced readers beyond the age of seven are potentially as capable as their peers in making affective and evaluative responses to text. In fact, children from both groups showed abilities commensurate with older children, although there were greater numbers of high responders in the Integrated Groups.

They are also capable of making informed judgements about literature and of choosing literature based on these judgements. Informed judgements can only be made if there is a range of styles and genres to choose from. Sensitive guidance from the teacher is usually necessary to encourage children to extend their choice and difficulty level. This means, of course, that teachers need to know about literature that is available for children at various levels.

Our research shows that children classified by schools as having reading difficulties are capable of discussing and recommending texts with reference to both author and title, if they have a range of literature to choose from. Children in the Schematic Groups were less able to do so, if their experience had been restricted to numbers and levels within reading schemes.

We concluded that some children, described by their schools as having difficulty with reading, actually spent far less time on reading than did other children. In some cases they avoided reading whenever they could in order to avoid associated failure. In others, they spent more time on 'words' out of context, sometimes in workbooks unrelated to the books they read. In yet other instances the focus was on testing reading rather than teaching strategies. Our research shows that inexperienced readers are capable of periods of sustained silent reading, if they are given the opportunity. If children do learn to read by reading, then these children have a right to as much, if not more, opportunity to read as their peers. They may need careful monitoring to ensure that books are read, although the results from our study suggest that, if choice of literature is a focus of classroom teaching, children are capable of choosing books that do sustain their interest and motivation to read. It is the responsibility of the teacher, language co-ordinator or head teacher to have within the classrooms as wide a range of 'quality' literature as possible so that real choices can be made. A reluctant reader is, after all 'any child for whom no adult has yet found suitable books.' (Jennings, 1992)

We have emphasised that an integrated approach to the teaching of reading to older, inexperienced readers does not negate teacher responsibilities or systematic teaching of strategies. On the contrary, it demands structure and organisation, a knowledge of the principles of teaching reading and knowledge of the range and content of literature suitable for individual children. So far schools have not always been successful in matching texts to readers or in providing texts which give both challenge and support. Successful implementation of an integrated approach requires that adults also communicate their own enthusiasm for reading as well as their confidence that inexperienced readers are capable of learning, given opportunity and systematic guidance.

Children in our Integrated Groups benefited from an approach which allowed them to take on some of the responsibility for their own learning. They have 'found' their books, as Jennings says, and they are developing a widening range of readerly behaviours to enable them to become more competent and committed. The same access to realising potential should be the entitlement of all children.

APPENDIX 1: Interview Guidance Questions

1. If you could spend time doing your favourite thing what would it be? (Demonstrate smiley face)
2. How about (i) TV (ii) playing on the computer (iii) drawing (iv) reading?
3. If you were offered these as birthday presents which would you choose (i) any book (ii) any computer game (iii) any video (iv) any board game?
4. Do you ever read at home? How often?
5. What do you read – comics, picture books, short stories, novels, rhymes?
6. What do you like most about them?
7. Is there anything you don't like to read? Why is that?
8. Where do you like to read? Why is that?
9. Do you prefer reading to yourself or to other people? Why is that?
10. If you have to read to other people who do you like to read to? Why is that? Who do you not like to read to? Why is that?
11. What do you find most difficult about reading?
12. What do you do if you're stuck on a word?
13. What would you like other people to do to help you?
14. Does anyone read to you?

APPENDIX 2: Intonation Examples

1. Brendan (Schematic Groups)

h
m r+   JUST he SPOKE // p   there CAME // r+   from the FORest a //
l

h   TERrible
m p   // p   ROAR // p   and the NEXT MOMent // o   a GREAT //
l

h
m p   LION // p   POUNced // p   INto // p   the ROAD // p   with ONE //
l

h
m p   BLOW //   p   of his PAW // p   he SENT THE // p   SCAREcrow
l

h
m SPINning // p   Over // p   and OVer // p   TO the EDGE // o   OF the //
l

h
m p   ROAD // o   and THEN he STUCK the // o   TIN // r+
l

h
m WOODMAN // o   WITH his // p   SHARP // p   CLAWS // o   BUT //
l

h
m TO the LION'S // r+   surPRISED // p   he COULDn't // p   MAKE //
l

h
m o   NO // p   imPRESSion // p   of the TIN //r   THOUGHTfully // r   the
l

h
m WOODman // r   FELL // o   OVer in the ROAD // p   and laid STILL //
l

2. Joseph (Integrated Groups)

```
h           IN                              ALways WEAR
m    // r+    FAIRy tales // p   WITCHes // p                    //
l
```

```
h
m    r+   SILLy black        // p   and BLACK          // o   AND //
l                  HATS                    CLOAKS
```

```
h            RIDE
m    r+   they       // r+   a BROOMstick // p   but THIS // p   is NOT //
l
```

```
h                                       REAL
m    p    a              // p   THIS is about        witches //
l         FAIRy tale
```

```
h
m    p   the MOST important THING you should KNOW // r+   about
l                                                           REAL
```

```
h                                                    NEVer
m    witches // p   is       // r   LISten // r+   VEry CAREfully // r+
l               THIS
```

```
h    forGET                          REAL WITches
m           // p   what is COMING NEXT // r+              //
l
```

```
h            ORdinary                 VERY MUCH
m    p   dress in        CLOTHES // p   look           //
l
```

```
h                                   ORdinary
m    p   like ORdinary WOMen // they LIVE in          HOUses // r   AND //
l
```

```
h                                        THAT
m    p   THEY // o   WORK // p   in ORdinary JOBS // r+        is WHY //
l
```

```
h
m   o    they ARE // r+   so HARD to CATCH // r+   a REAL witch // r+
l
```

```
                             RED hot
h
m   HATES children // p    with a         // p   SIZZling HATE // r+   that is
l
```

```
h   MORE                              ANY
m        sizzling and red hot // r+   than      hate you could POSSibly //
l
```

```
h
m   p   iMAGine
l
```

References

Adams, M.J. (1990) *Beginning to Read: Thinking and Learning about Print.* London: MIT Press.

Ahlberg, J. and Ahlberg, A. (1982) *The Ha Ha Bonk Book.* Harmondsworth: Puffin.

Ahlberg, J. and Ahlberg, A. (1986) *The Jolly Postman or Other People's Letters.* London: Heinemann.

Aiken, J. (1977) 'The Pirate Parrot Princess' in A. Wood (ed.) *Stories for Children.* London: Hodder and Stoughton.

Allington, R.L. (1983) 'The Reading Instruction provided for readers of differing reading abilities', *The Elementary School Journal*, 1983, pp. 548–559.

Arnold, H. (1990) 'Making Reading Real', in P.D. Pumfrey and C.D. Elliot (eds) *Children's Difficulties in Reading, Spelling and Writing.* Basingstoke: The Falmer Press.

Assessment of Performance Unit (1987) *Pupils' Attitudes to Reading at Age 11 and 15* (T. Gorman). Windsor: NFER-Nelson.

Ausubel, D. (1971) *School Learning: an introduction to Educational Psychology.* London: Holt, Rinehart and Winston.

Baker, A. (1984) 'Choice and Availability of Books' in NATE *Children reading to their teachers.* Sheffield: National Association for the Teaching of English.

Barr, R.C. (1972) 'The influence of instructional conditions on word recognition errors', *Reading Research Quarterly*, **7**, pp.509–529.

Barrett, P., Barrs, M., Bibby, B., Dombey, H., Furlong, T. and Scott, P. (1989) *Learning to be literate in a Democratic Society.* Sheffield: National Association for the Teaching of English.

Beech, J.R. (1985) *Learning to Read: A Cognitive Approach to Reading and Poor Reading.* London: Croom Helm.

Beech, J.R. (1987) 'Early Reading Development' in J. Beech and A. Colley (eds) *Cognitive Approaches to Reading.* Chichester: John Wiley and Sons.

Bennett, J. (1985) *Learning to read with Picture Books* (3rd edn). Stroud: Thimble Press.

Berry, C. (1975) *Your Voice: How to Use it Successfully.* London: Harrap.

Bettelheim, B. (1976) *The Use of Enchantment: The meaning and importance of fairy tales.* London: Thames and Hudson.

Bettelheim, B. and Zelan, K. (1991) *On Learning to Read: the child's fascination with meaning.* London: Penguin.

Blank, M. (1985) 'The Relationship between Oral and Written Language' in

M.M. Clark (ed.) *New Directions in the Study of Reading*. Lewes: The Falmer Press.

Bloom, W., Martin, T. and Walters, M. (1988) *Managing to Read: a whole school approach to reading*. London: Mary Glasgow Publications.

Bradley, L. (1990) 'Rhyming Connections in Learning' in P.D. Pumfrey and C.D. Elliot (eds) *Children's Difficulties in Reading, Spelling and Writing*. Basingstoke: The Falmer Press.

Braun, F.G. (1985) 'Reading problems related to teaching', *Reading*, **19**, No. 1, pp.20–23.

Brazil, D., Coulthard, M. and Jones, C. (1980) *Discourse Intonation and Language Teaching*. London: Longman Group Ltd.

Briggs, R. (1980) *The Snowman*. Harmondsworth: Puffin.

Bruner, J.S. (1966) *Towards a Theory of Instruction*. Cambridge, Mass.: Belknapp Press of Harvard University.

Bruner, J.S. (1977) *The Process of Education: A searching discussion of school education opening new paths to teaching and learning*. Harvard: Harvard University Press.

Bruner, J.S. (1986) *Actual Minds, Possible Worlds*. Cambridge, Mass.: Harvard University Press.

Bryant, P. and Bradley, L. (1985) *Children's Reading Problems: Psychology and Education*. Oxford: Blackwell.

Burningham, J. (1977) *Come Away from the Water, Shirley*. London: Jonathan Cape.

Burt, C. (1974) *Burt Reading Test*. Scottish Council for Research in Education.

Butzow, C. and Butzow, J. (1988) 'Importance of Story' in C. Anderson (ed.) *Reading: the abc and Beyond*. Basingstoke: Macmillan.

Cadman, B.W. (1983) 'Pupils reading: a case study of a catchment area', unpublished M.Ed. Thesis (University of Birmingham) cited in B. Wade 'A Picture of Reading', *Educational Review*, **38**, No. 1, pp.3–9

Cairney, T.H. (1990) *Teaching Reading Comprehension*. Milton Keynes: Open University Press.

Campbell, R. (1986) 'Social Relationships in Hearing Children Read', *Reading*, **20**, 3, pp.157–167.

Cashdan, A. and Pumfrey, P. (1969) 'Some effects of remedial teaching in reading', *Educational Research*, **11**, No. 7, pp.138–147.

Cateldo, S. and Ellis, N. (1990) 'Learning to Spell, Learning to Read' in P.D. Pumfrey and C.D. Elliot (eds) *Children's Difficulties in Reading, Spelling and Writing*. Basingstoke: The Falmer Press.

Cazden, C.B. (1979) 'The neglected situation in child language' in V. Lee (ed.) *Language Development*. London: Croom Helm.

Chall, J. (1983) *Learning to Read: The Great Debate* (2nd edn). New York: McGraw Hill Inc.

Chall, J.S., Jacobs, V.A. and Baldwin, L.E. (1990) *The Reading Crisis: Why poor children fall behind*. Cambridge, Mass.: Harvard University Press.

Chambers, A. (1981) (ed.) *The Signal Approach to Children's Books*. Metuchen, N.J.: Scarecrow Press.

120

Chambers, A. (1985) *Booktalk*. London: The Bodley Head.

Chambers, A. (1991) *The Reading Environment*. Stroud: The Thimble Press.

Chapman, J. (1987) *Reading from 5-11 years*. Milton Keynes: Open University Press.

Choate, J.S. and Rakes, T.A. (1989) *Reading, Detecting and Correcting Special Needs*. Boston: Allyn and Bacon Inc.

Clay, M.M. (1979) *Reading: The Patterning of Complex Behaviour* (2nd edn). Auckland: Heinemann.

Cohen, L. and Manion, L. (1989) (3rd edn) *Research Methods in Education*. London: Routledge.

Cole, B (1985) *The Trouble With Mum*. London: Picture Lions, Collins.

Collins, J.E. (1961) *The Effects of Remedial Education*. London: Oliver and Boyd.

Corcoran, B. and Evans, E. (1987) (eds) *Readers, Texts, Teachers*. Milton Keynes: Open University Press.

Crossley, M. and Vulliamy, G. (1984) 'Case Study research methods and comparative education', *Comparative Education*, **20**, pp.193–207.

Dahl, R. (1967) *Charlie and the Chocolate Factory*. London: Allen and Unwin.

Dahl, R. (1981) *George's Marvellous Medicine*. Harmondsworth: Puffin.

Daneman, M. (1987) 'Reading and Working Memory' in J.R. Beech and A.M. Colley (eds) *Cognitive Approaches to Reading*. Chichester: John Wiley and Sons.

Deci, E.L., Sheinman, L., Schwartz, A.J. and Ryan, R.M. (1981) 'An instrument to assess adults' orientation towards control versus autonomy with children', *Journal of Educational Psychology*, **73**, pp.642–650.

Department For Education and Welsh Office (1995) *English in the National Curriculum*. London: HMSO.

Department of Education and Science (1975) *A Language for Life* (Bullock Report). London: HMSO.

Department of Education and Science (1990) *The Teaching and Learning of Language and Literacy* (HMI Report). London: HMSO.

Department of Education and Science and Welsh Office (1988) *English for Ages 5–11* (Cox Report). London: HMSO.

Department of Education and Science and Welsh Office (1989) *English for Ages 5–16* (Cox Report). London: HMSO.

Department of Education and Science and Welsh Office (1990) *English in the National Curriculum*. London: HMSO.

Department of Education and Science and Welsh Office (1991) *The Teaching and Learning of Reading in Primary Schools*. London: HMSO.

Dombey, H. (1992) 'Lessons Learnt at Bedtime' in K. Kimberley, M. Meek and J. Miller (eds) *New Readings: Contributions to an understanding of literacy*. London: A & C Black.

Donaldson, M. (1989) *Sense and Sensibility – Some thoughts on the teaching of literacy*, Occasional Paper No. 3. Reading and Language Information Centre: University of Reading.

Dupasquier, P. (1990) *I Can't Sleep*. London: Walker Books.

Durkin, D. (1965) *Children who read early*. New York: Teachers College Press.

Evans, K.M. (1965) *Attitudes and Interests in Education*. London: Routledge and Kegan Paul.

Findlay, W. (1986) 'Why Can't I Read?', *Reading*, **20**, No. 1, pp.53–58.

Froese, V. (1991) 'The Research Basis of Whole Language'. Talk given at the Language and Literacy International Convention, University of East Anglia, Norwich, 8 April.

Fry, D. (1985) *Children Talk About Books: Seeing themselves as readers*. Milton Keynes: Open University Press.

Goodacre, E.J. (1971) *Children and Learning to Read*. London: Routledge and Kegan Paul.

Goodman, K.S. (1986) *What's Whole in Whole Language*. Ontario: Scholastic–TAB.

Goodman, K.S. (1992) 'I didn't found whole language', *The Reading Teacher*, **46**, pp.188–199.

Harding, L.M., Beech, J.R. and Sneddon, W. (1985) 'The changing pattern of reading errors and reading style from 5-11 years of age', *British Journal of Educational Psychology*, **55**, pp.45–52.

Harrison, C. (1979) 'Assessing the Readability of School Texts' in E. Lunzer and K. Gardner (eds) *The Effective Use of Reading*. London: Heinemann.

Hayhoe, M. and Parker, S. (eds) (1990) *Reading and Response*. Milton Keynes: Open University Press.

Holdaway, D. (1980) (2nd edn) *Independence in Reading*. Gosford: Ashton Scholastic.

Hudson, J. (1988) 'Real Books for Real Readers for Real Purposes', *Reading*, **22**, pp.78–83.

Hughes, V.M. (1991) Literature Belongs to Everyone – A report on widening access to literature. London: Arts Council of Great Britain.

Huxford, L., Terrell, C. and Bradley, L. (1991) 'The relationship between the phonological strategies employed in reading and spelling', *Journal of Research in Reading*, **14**, No. 2, pp.99–105.

ILEA (1988) *Primary Language Record*, M. Barrs, C. Ellis, H. Hester and A. Thomas. London: Centre for Language in Primary Language.

Imai, M., Anderson, R.C., Wilkinson, I.A.G. and Yi, H. (1992) 'Properties of attention during reading lessons', *Journal of Educational Psychology*, **84**, pp.160–173.

Iser, W. (1978) *The act of reading: A theory of aesthetic response*. London: Routledge and Kegan Paul.

James, S. (1991) *Dear Greenpeace*. London: Walker Books.

Jansen, M. (1985) 'Language and Concepts' in M.M. Clark (ed.) *New Directions in the Study of Reading*. Lewes: The Falmer Press.

Jennings, P. (1992) quoted in *The Bookseller*, p.1500, 13 November.

Kohl, H. (1988) (rev edn) *Reading, How to*. Milton Keynes: Open University Press.

Labov, W. (1970) 'The Logic of non-standard English' in F. Williams (ed.) *Language and Poverty*. Chicago: Markham Publishing Co.

Lapp, D. and Flood, J. (1978) *Teaching Reading to Every Child*. New York: Macmillan.

Lavender, R. (1985) 'The Quality of Story' in B. Root (ed.) *Resources for Reading: Does Quality Count?* Basingstoke: Macmillan.

Lowndes, A. and Hunter-Carsch, M. (1989) 'Language and Art: enhancing reading comprehension by re-routing words through creating visual images' in M. Hunter-Carsch (ed.) *The Art of Reading*. Oxford: Blackwell.

Lutrario, C. (1990) *Hooked on Books, Children's reading fiction*. London: Harcourt Brace Jovanovich.

Martin, T. (1989) *The Strugglers: Working with children who fail to read*. Milton Keynes: Open University Press.

Martin, T. (1993) 'Reading as if for Life', *Reading*, **27**, pp.26–31.

McKinlay, S. (1990) 'Children's Attitudes to Reading: Do teachers know?', *Reading*, **24**, No. 3, pp.166–178.

Meek, M. (1982) *Learning to Read*. London: The Bodley Head.

Meek, M. (1983) *Achieving Literacy*. London: Routledge and Kegan Paul.

Meek, M. (1988) *How Texts Teach What Readers Learn*. Stroud: Thimble Press.

Meek, M. (1989) 'What do we know about reading that helps us to teach it?', *Language and Learning*, **1**, pp.2–8.

Merriam, S.B. (1988) *Case Study Approach in Education: A Qualitative Approach*. San Francisco: Jossey Bass.

Merritt, J. (1985) 'The Intermediate Skills Revisited' in M.M. Clark (ed.) *New Directions in the Study of Reading*. Lewes: The Falmer Press.

Michael, I. (1987) *The Teaching of English from the Sixteenth Century to 1870*. Cambridge: Cambridge University Press.

Minns, H. (1990) *Read It To Me Now! Learning at Home and at School*. London: Virago.

Moon, C. (1988) 'Reading: where are we now?' in M. Meek and C. Mills (eds) *Language and Literacy in the Primary School*. Lewes: The Falmer Press.

Moon, C. *Individualised Reading*. Centre for the Teaching of Reading: University of Reading. (Revised annually.)

Moon, C. and Raban-Bisby, B. (1992) (3rd edn) *A Question of Reading*. London: David Fulton.

Moore, M. and Wade, B. (1994) 'Accounting and Providing for Struggling Readers', *CORE*, **18**, No. 2.

Moore, M. and Wade, B. (1995) 'Reading and Reading Failure: Perspectives on general and remedial provision', *CORE*, **19**, No. 1.

Murphy, J. (1982) *On the Way Home*. London: Macmillan.

Myers, S.S. (1991) 'Performance in Reading Comprehension – product or process?', *Educational Review*, **43**, No. 3, pp.257–272.

Naidoo, S. (1981) 'Teaching Methods and their Rationale' in G. Pavlidis and T.R. Miles (eds) *Dyslexia Research and its Application to Education*. Chichester: John Wiley and Sons.

National Curriculum Council (1989) Curriculum Guidance 2 *A Curriculum For All: Special Educational Needs in the National Curriculum*. York: NCC.

National Oracy Project (1990) *Teaching Talking and Learning in Key Stage 1.* York: NCC.

National Oracy Project (1991) *Teaching Talking and Learning in Key Stage 2.* York: NCC.

Naughton, W. (1968) 'Seventeen Oranges' in *The Goalkeeper's Revenge and Other Stories.* Harmondsworth: Puffin.

Neale, M. (1966 and 1989) (2nd edn) *Neale Analysis of Reading Ability.* Basingstoke: Macmillan.

NFER (1970) Reading Test AD. Windsor: National Foundation for Educational Research.

Nomiku, F. (1991) *Young children's reading in context: case studies of 5-8 year olds reading in a primary school classroom.* Unpublished PhD Thesis: University of East Anglia.

Peters, M.L. and Smith, B. (1985) 'The Productive Process: An Approach to Literacy for Children with Difficulties' in B. Root (ed.) *Resources for Reading: Does Quality Count?* Basingstoke: Macmillan.

Phillips, M. (1990) 'Educashun still isn't working', *Guardian*, 28 September.

Pinsett, P. (1990) *Children with Literacy Difficulties.* London: David Fulton Publishers.

Powney, J. and Watts, M. (1987) *Interviewing in Educational Research.* London: Routledge and Kegan Paul.

Prater, J. (1987) *The Gift.* Harmondsworth: Puffin.

Protherough, R. (1983) *Developing Response to Fiction.* Milton Keynes: Open University Press.

Roberts, T. (1989) 'Learning to Read: developing understanding', *Reading,* **23**, No. 1, pp.9–16.

Simmons, K. (1987) 'Children's Story Telling: what it can tell us about reading difficulties', *Reading,* **9**, No. 4, pp.555–567.

Simmons, K. (1991) 'Reading Recovery: what does it have to offer UK schools?', *Reading,* **25**, No. 3, pp.22–25.

Skinner, B.F. (1969) *Contingencies of Reinforcement: A theoretical analysis.* New York: Appleton-Century-Crofts.

Skinner, B.F. (1972) *Beyond Freedom and Dignity.* London: Jonathan Cape.

Slim, J. (1990) 'The Write Stuff', *Evening Mail*, Birmingham, 28 November.

Smith, F. (1973) *Psycholinguistics and Reading.* New York: Holt, Rinehart and Winston.

Smith, F. (1982) (3rd edn) *Understanding Reading.* New York: CBS College Publishing, Holt, Rinehart and Winston.

Smith, F. (1988) *Joining the Literacy Club.* Portsmouth, NH: Heinemann.

Smith, F. (1991) 'Literacy: Understanding and Obstacles. We learn from the company we keep'. Talk given at the Language and Literacy International Convention, University of East Anglia, Norwich, 7 April.

Somerfield, M., Torbe, M. and Wood, C. (1983) *A Framework for Reading.* London: Heinemann.

Southgate, V. (1973) 'The Language Arts in Informal British Primary Schools', *The Reading Teacher,* **26**, No. 4, pp.367–373.

Southgate, V. (1985) 'Teachers of Reading: planning for the most effective use of their time' in B. Root (ed.) *Resources for Reading: Does Quality Count?* Basingstoke: Macmillan.

Southgate, V., Arnold, H. and Johnson, S. (1981) *Extending Beginning Reading*. London: Heinemann.

Spencer, M. (1976) 'Stories are for Telling', *English in Education*, **10**, No. 1, pp.16–23.

Squire, J.R. (1990) 'Research on Reader Response and the National Literature Initiative' in M. Hayhoe and S. Parker *Reading and Response*. Milton Keynes: Open University Press.

Stake, R.E. (1981) 'Case Study Methodology: An Epistemological Advocacy' in W.W. Welsh (ed.) *Case Study Methodology in Educational Evaluation*, Proceedings of the 1981 Minnesota Evaluation Conference. Minneapolis: Minnesota Research and Evaluation Centre.

Stein, N.L. and Glenn, C.G. (1979) 'An analysis of story comprehension in elementary school children' in R.O. Freedle (ed.) *Advances in Discourse Processes, Vol 2 New Directions in Discourse Processing*. Norwood, NJ: Ablex.

Tansley, A.E. (1976) *Sound Sense*. Leeds: E. J. Arnold.

Tansley, A.E. and Nicholls, R.H. (1962) *Racing to Read*. Leeds: E. J. Arnold & Sons Ltd.

Thomson, J. (1987) *Understanding Teenagers' Reading*. Adelaide: Australian Association for the Teaching of English.

Thomson, J. (1992) (ed.) *Reconstructing Literature Teaching: New Essays on the Teaching of Literature*. Norwood: Australian Association for the Teaching of English.

Thorndike, E.L. (1931) *Human Learning*. New York: Prentice Hall.

Tindall, W. (1986) 'Children's Literature: A perspective', *Early Child Development and Care*, **26**, pp.209–215.

Tonjes, M.J. (1988) 'Monitoring Comprehension is what skilled readers do' in C. Anderson (ed.) *Reading: the abc and Beyond*. Basingstoke: Macmillan.

Verma, G.K. and Beard, R.M. (1981) *What is Educational Research? Perspectives on Techniques of Research*. Aldershot: Gower Publishing Company.

Vygotsky, L.S. (1962) *Thought and Language*. Cambridge, Mass.: Harvard University Press.

Vygotsky, L.S. (1978) *Mind in Society*. Cambridge, Mass.: Harvard University Press.

Wade, B. (1984) *Story at Home and School*, Educational Review Ocasional Publications 10, University of Birmingham.

Wade, B. (1990) *Reading for Real*. Milton Keynes: Open University Press.

Wade, B. and Cadman, B.W. (1986) 'Readers at Risk', *Educational Review*, **43**, No. 2, pp.23–29.

Wade, B. and Moore, M. (1992) *Patterns of Educational Integration: International Perspectives on Mainstreaming Children with Special Educational Needs*. Wallingford: Triangle Books.

Wade, B. and Moore, M. (1993) *The Promise of Reading Recovery.* Headline Series 1, Educational Review, University of Birmingham.

Wade, B. and Moore, M. (1993a) *Experiencing Special Education.* Buckingham: Open University Press.

Wade, B., Wade, A. and Moore, M. (1988) 'Fair is Fair' in *Eastern Promise.* Walton-on-Thames: Thomas Nelson and Sons.

Waterland, L. (1988) *Read With Me: An Apprenticeship Approach to Reading* (2nd edn). Stroud: Thimble Press.

Weaver, C. (1992) *Psycholinguistics and Reading: From Process to Practice.* Cambridge, Mass.: Winthrop.

Whitehead, F., Capey, A.C., Madden, W. and Wellings, A. (1977) *Children and their Books.* Basingstoke: Macmillan.

Wood, D. (1988) *How Children Think and Learn.* Oxford: Blackwell.

Woods, P. (1990) *The Happiest Days?* London: The Falmer Press.

Yin, R.K. (1989) *Case Study Research: Design and Methods* (rev. edn). Newbury Park: Sage Publications.

Zigler, C., Abelson, W.D. and Seitz, V. (1973) 'Motivational Factors in the Performance of Economically Disadvantaged Children on the Peabody Picture Vocabulary Test', *Child Development*, **44**, pp.294–303.

INDEX

130
USSR 108

visual memory 7
Vygotsky, Lev 79

word attack 4, 5
word attack skills 19
word building 107
word recognition 2, 4, 6, 19–21
word shape 2, 6, 15, 17
writing 4, 5, 9–10, 80, 81–83, 94–100